# Excel for Windows™ Hot Tips

**Ron Person**

*Excel for Windows Hot Tips*

Copyright© 1993 by Que® Corporation

Library of Congress Catalog No.: 93-83024

ISBN: 1-56529-164-6

96  95  94  93     4  3  2  1

Interpretation of the printing code: the rightmost double-digit number is the year of the book's printing; the rightmost single-digit number, the number of the book's printing. For example, a printing code of 93-1 shows that the first printing of the book occurred in 1993.

# Credits

**Publisher**
Lloyd J. Short

**Associate Publisher**
Rick Ranucci

**Operations Manager**
Sheila Cunningham

**Publishing Plan Manager**
Thomas H. Bennett

**Title Manager**
Shelley O'Hara

**Product Director**
Joyce J. Nielsen
Robin Drake

**Acquisitions Editor**
Chris Katsaropoulos

**Production Editors**
Jodi Jensen
Anne Owen
Susan Pink

**Technical Editor**
Lynda Fox

**Production Team**
Claudia Bell
Julie Brown
Jodie Cantwell
Paula Carroll
Laurie Casey
Brad Chinn
Michelle Cleary
Brook Farling
Heather Kaufman
Bob LaRoche
Linda Seifert
Phil Worthington

**Indexer**
Joy Dean Lee
Tina Trettin

Composed in *Utopia* and *MCPdigital* by Prentice Hall Computer Publishing

# About the Authors

**Ron Person** is one of the original Microsoft Consulting Partners, Microsoft's highest rating for Microsoft Excel and Word for Windows consultants. He has written more than a dozen books for Que Corporation, including *Using Excel 4 for Windows*, Special Edition; *Using Windows 3.1*, Special Edition; and *Using Word for Windows 2*, Special Edition, and is the coauthor of Que's *Using Access for Windows*. He has an M.S. in physics from Ohio State University and an M.B.A. from Hardin-Simmons University.

Ron is the principal consultant for Ron Person & Co., one of the leading developers and trainers in Microsoft Excel. The company has been developing stand-alone and client-server applications using Microsoft Excel since 1989. Their applications aid corporations in the areas of finance, marketing, human resources, and Enterprise Information Systems (EIS). They train and support corporate developers nationwide in Microsoft Excel macros, Microsoft Access macros, and BASIC. For information on application development or on-site classes for your corporation, contact

Ron Person & Co.
P.O. Box 5647
3 Quixote Court
Santa Rosa, CA 95409

| | |
|---|---|
| 415-989-7508 | Voice |
| 707-539-1525 | Voice |
| 707-538-1485 | Fax |

# Table of Contents

# Introduction

Whether you are a beginning or experienced Excel for Windows user, the shortcuts and powerful techniques in *Excel for Windows Hot Tips* will help improve your proficiency. In this book you find information about the subtle program features you were too busy to read about in the documentation. You also find secrets, undocumented tips, and proven advice.

Each chapter includes tips for a particular feature or function of Excel for Windows. For example, the toolbar tips are in the "Using Toolbars" chapter, and the printing tips are in the "Printing and Page Layout" chapter. Unlike some computer books, the chapters and tips in this book do not need to be read in any particular order.

 Watch for tips identified by a "Hot" icon. These tips are the author's favorites and are bound to pique your interest. You can find a list of these tips on the inside front and back covers.

If you want a comprehensive overview of Excel for Windows, pick up a copy of Que's *Using Excel 4 for Windows*, Special Edition.

## Book Conventions

The conventions in *Excel for Windows Hot Tips* will help you understand the techniques described in the text. This section provides examples of these conventions.

Words printed in uppercase include Excel functions (such as DATE) and file names (such as CHANGER.XLA). The following table shows the special formatting used in this book.

| Format | Meaning |
| --- | --- |
| *italics* | Emphasized text and variables |
| **boldface** | Hot keys for menu options and information the reader types |
| `special typeface` | Direct quotations of words that appear on-screen or in a figure; menu command prompts |

Keys are represented as they appear on most keyboards. The Control key is abbreviated Ctrl, Page Up is PgUp, Insert is Ins, and so on. The term *Enter* is used instead of *Return* for the Enter key.

Key combinations shown with a + (plus sign) indicate that you press the keys at the same time. To enter the Shift+F10 combination, for example, press and hold the Shift key while you press the F10 key. If a key combination is shown without a plus (for example, End Home), don't hold down any of the keys; press each key once in the order listed.

# 1

# Working with Files and Workbooks

Understanding how to efficiently work with Microsoft Excel files can help you with such things as creating a startup worksheet, opening multiple files at one time, and removing unused space from files. Workbooks are new to Excel 4. They enable you to group multiple worksheets, charts, and macro sheets into one file. This packaging of work into a single book can make it easier to work with some multiple file projects.

## Open a document automatically on startup

When Excel starts, it automatically opens any worksheet, macro, or chart file if you place it in the \EXCEL\XLSTART directory. When you no longer want this file to open automatically, delete or remove it from the \XLSTART subdirectory.

## Create a custom startup worksheet

 You can create a custom startup worksheet that contains the styles, named ranges, formulas, and settings you use most frequently. Each new worksheet you open will contain your custom settings.

To create your own default startup worksheet:

1. Modify a new or existing worksheet so it contains all the settings, text, numbers, formats, styles, and formulas you need. Make the worksheet exactly as you want it to appear when you start Excel or choose File New.

2. Choose the File Save As command to display the Save As dialog box.

3. Type the file name **SHEET** in the File Name edit box.

4. Select Template from the Save File as Type pull-down list. This action changes the file extension to XLT.

5. Change to the \EXCEL\XLSTART directory, then choose OK. This action saves your worksheet as a template named SHEET.XLT in the XLSTART directory.

Excel opens your SHEET.XLT template and adds a numeric suffix so the sheet title appears as Sheet1 on startup. Each new worksheet you open will show Sheet followed by the number of new worksheets that have been opened during that work session, for example, Sheet2, Sheet3, and so on.

## Start Excel without a startup worksheet

Start Excel 3 or Excel 4 without a startup worksheet by using the /E switch in Excel's startup command line. To do so:

1. Activate the Program Manager and select the Excel program icon.

2. Choose the File Properties command or press Alt+Enter to display the Program Item Properties dialog box.

3. The Command Line edit box contains the path and file name to start Excel, for example, C:\EXCEL\EXCEL.EXE. Add /E to the end of the command line, as shown in figure 1.1.

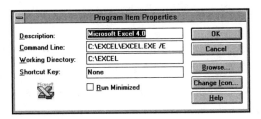

**Fig. 1.1**  *Command line to start Excel without a worksheet.*

## Create templates that appear in the File New dialog box

*Templates* are files that act as patterns on which to base new worksheets, macro sheets, or charts. A worksheet or macro sheet template can contain styles, column widths, text, numbers, formulas, names, custom formats, and so on. It might be a finished worksheet except for the data values that need to be entered. A chart template contains all the formatting and settings used for a chart, but it contains no data.

If you need a template for a worksheet, macro sheet, or chart you use repetitively, consider creating a template as described in the following steps. New sheets opened from a template must be saved to a new name, thus protecting the original template from being overwritten.

Another advantage is that templates saved in the XLSTART directory appear in the New dialog box when you choose the File New command. This action makes a template readily available no matter what directory you are in currently.

To create a worksheet, macro sheet, or chart template:

1. Create the worksheet, macro sheet, or chart containing all the contents and formatting you want in the template.

2. Save the worksheet, macro sheet, or chart as a template by choosing the File Save As command.

3. In the File Name edit box, type the name by which you want to recognize the template.

4. Select Template from the Save File as Type pull-down list.

5. Change to the XLSTART directory under the EXCEL directory. Choose OK.

Templates can be saved to and opened from any directory, but templates in the \EXCEL\XLSTART directory will appear in the New dialog box.

## Open multiple files at the same time

Opening many files from the same directory takes a while if you open them one at a time. You can, however, open multiple files at once. With the Open dialog box displayed, you can open files that are adjacent in the list by clicking the topmost file, then holding down the Shift key as you click the lowest file in the list you want selected. The two files you clicked and all files in between are selected. Choose OK or press Enter to open all the selected files.

If you want to select multiple nonadjacent files, click one file, then hold down the Ctrl key as you click other files. Choose OK or press Enter to open the selected files.

## Close all files at the same time

You can close all open files at one time. To do so, hold down the Shift key as you choose the File menu. The command Close All replaces the Close command. Choose Close All to close all open worksheets, macro sheets, and charts. You are prompted with a request to save files that have changed since they were initially opened. The Global macro and add-in macros are not closed.

## Use a timed reminder to save files

One of Excel's add-ins is an autosave feature that reminds you to save your work. When you add this feature, it appears in your normal Excel menu as the Options AutoSave command. When you choose this command, the AutoSave dialog box shown in figure 1.2 appears. When AutoSave is on, a check mark appears next to the AutoSave command in the menu.

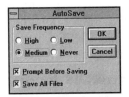

**Fig. 1.2**  *Use AutoSave to remind yourself to save your work.*

If the AutoSave command does not appear in the Options menu, you need to add the AutoSave add-in. To do this:

1. Choose the Options Add-ins command.

2. Choose the Add button, then open the AUTOSAVE.XLA file.

3. Choose the Close button to return to your worksheet.

If the AUTOSAVE.XLA file does not appear in the
EXCEL\LIBRARY directory, repeat the Excel installation
process but choose the Custom installation and install
only the add-in files.

## Send multiple files as a single document

When you need to pass multiple Excel documents to another Excel user, it can be more convenient to put all the
documents into a workbook. This reduces the chance that
a file will be forgotten. It also makes it easier to send electronic mail.

To collect multiple documents into a single file, you must
bind the documents into a workbook. Choose File New,
select Workbook from the list, and choose OK. This opens
a blank workbook. Bind documents into the workbook by
clicking the Add button. If you want to bind a document
that is not open, choose the Open button, select the document, and choose OK. Bound documents appear on the
workbook contents page with an icon of stacked pages.

## Remove documents from a workbook

To remove a document from the workbook, first display
the contents page by clicking the content icon in the lower
right corner of the workbook. Then select the file from the
contents page and choose the Remove button.

## Use long, readable names in workbook documents

One advantage to binding documents into a workbook
is that you can give the documents longer and more

readable names. To give a bound document a more readable name:

1. Select the document from the workbook index.

2. Choose the Document Options button to display the Options dialog box.

3. In the **Document Name** edit box, type the name you want for this document. Names can be up to 31 characters and can contain spaces.

Note that if you unbind a document, you must shorten a long name to a name acceptable by DOS.

## Control your workbook with keystrokes

The buttons in the workbook contents page do not appear to be accessible by keystrokes, but they are. Use the following keystrokes to activate these buttons:

| | |
|---|---|
| Shift+Alt+A | Add button |
| Shift+Alt+R | Remove button |
| Shift+Alt+O | Options button |

The buttons are activated with the mouse by clicking.

## Right-click to move between workbook pages

You can use the mouse to move between workbook pages quickly. First, click the right mouse button on one of the three page icons at the lower right corner of a workbook document. When the workbook shortcut menu displays the available documents, click the document you want to activate.

## Use group edit to make the same edits in documents in a workbook

If you need to make the same changes in multiple documents in a workbook, use Excel's group edit feature. To quickly select the documents you want to edit together:

1. Switch to the workbook contents page, then select the documents you want to edit using Ctrl+click.

2. Choose the **O**ptions **G**roup Edit command.

3. When the Group Edit dialog box appears, choose OK. (The correct documents are already selected.)

## Move or remove multiple documents from a workbook

You can select multiple documents on the workbook contents page and then move or remove all the selected documents. To select multiple documents that are adjacent in the list, click the first document name, then hold down the Shift key as you click the last in your selection. To select multiple documents that are not adjacent, click one of the document names, then hold down the Ctrl key as you click each additional document name.

To move multiple selected documents, drag them to a new location in the workbook contents list. To remove all the selected documents, choose the **R**emove button.

## Click to bind or unbind workbook documents

Bind or unbind documents from the workbook by switching to the workbook's contents page. Click the icon at the right of the contents page to toggle the document between bound and unbound. An icon that shows a stack of pages indicates a bound document. An icon that shows a stack with loose pages is unbound.

## Store summary information about a worksheet

You may be able to manage your worksheets better if you use Excel's Summary add-in. The Summary dialog box appears in figure 1.3. The dialog box invisibly stores in the worksheet summary information such as the date the sheet was created, the revision number, and comments. By storing the information in hidden names, the worksheet remains clean of extraneous information.

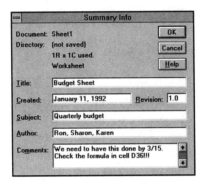

**Fig. 1.3**   *Use the Summary add-in to help manage document versions.*

To use the summary information feature, you must install the Summary add-in, as follows:

1. Choose the Options Add-ins command.

2. The Add-In Manager dialog box appears. Choose the Add button.

3. The File Open dialog box appears. Select the SUMMARY.XLA file, which is usually found in the EXCEL\LIBRARY directory, then choose OK.

4. The Add-In Manager dialog box returns, with Document Summary in the Add-Ins Installed list. Choose the Close button unless you want to add other add-ins to Excel.

*Working with Files and Workbooks*   **11**

The Document Summary add-in is now available whenever you run Excel. To remove the Document Summary add-in, reopen the Add-In Manager, select the Document Summary add-in, and choose the **Remove** button.

When you want to edit or review the summary information, choose Edit Summary Info. Edit the information in any of the edit boxes. You cannot change the creation date, however.

## Remove unused space from your worksheets

Excel may use more memory than is actually needed by your worksheet. This can cause problems if you use a system with very little memory or if you load many worksheets or applications at one time. If you format large areas outside the used portion of the worksheet, for example, or enter data far away from the main body of the worksheet and then move it close to the main body, Excel may reserve more memory than the worksheet needs.

Excel reserves memory for large blocks of the worksheet. To find where Excel thinks the lower right corner of the reserved block is, press Ctrl+End. This action selects the lowest right cell in the used portion of the worksheet. If this cell is far from the lowest right cell that contains data or a formula, you are probably wasting memory and file storage space.

To free up excess memory used by the worksheet:

1. Find the lower right corner of the memory block that Excel has set aside by pressing Ctrl+Enter.

2. Select all the rows below the last row that contains data or formulas, then choose Edit Delete. Select rows by dragging down across the letters in the row headings. If you are using the keyboard, press Shift+spacebar, then hold down the Shift key as you press the down arrow key. (Edit Clear will not work. Clearing only removes the cell contents or formats but does not remove the cell locations from memory.)

3. Select all the columns to the right of the last column that contains data or formulas, then choose Edit Delete. (Edit Clear will not work.)

4. Choose File Save and save the worksheet.

5. Close the worksheet.

6. Choose File Open and reopen the worksheet.

By deleting the rows and columns below and to the right of the actual worksheet, you tell Excel to remove them from the worksheet. Excel does not reallocate the memory, however, until you close the worksheet and reopen it.

# 2

**CHAPTER**

# Moving and Selecting Data

It's easy to move the active cell and select a cell or range, but many tricks in Excel make the process even easier or faster. In this chapter, you learn how to select a frequently used range at the press of a key, see each of the corners in a large selection, and move across large areas of the worksheet quickly. Some of the most time-saving tips are simple accessibility tips. One of the most favorite accessibility tips is using the shortcut menus.

## Use the mouse to access shortcut menus

 If you use a mouse, you will want to use shortcut menus immediately. Shortcut menus, like the ones shown in figures 2.1 and 2.2, enable you to quickly get to commands associated with the object you clicked. For example, pointing to a cell and clicking the right mouse button displays a menu of commands related to modifying a cell. Pointing to a column in a chart and clicking the right mouse button displays a menu of commands related to modifying a column.

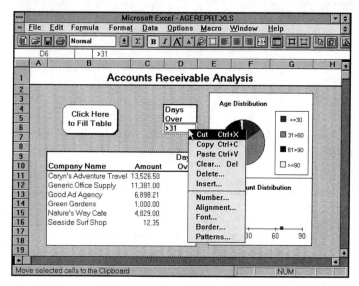

**Fig. 2.1**  *Use shortcut menus to choose the commands associated with the object you click.*

Shortcut menus appear beneath the pointer. To access a shortcut menu, point to the object (for example, a cell or column), then click and hold the right mouse button. The shortcut menu appears beneath the pointer. Drag down to the command, then release the mouse button.

A similar way to access a shortcut menu is to point to the object, then click and release the right mouse button. When the shortcut menu appears, click the command with the left mouse button.

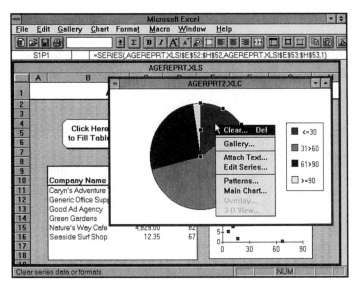

**Fig. 2.2** *Use shortcut menus to format charts more quickly.*

## Use Ctrl+Enter to fill cells with formulas or data

You can enter data or formulas and fill cells at the same time. With this technique, you are filling cells with data or formulas at the same time you enter the data or formulas. This saves you the steps normally needed for the fill or copy and paste commands.

To fill data or formulas into cells or a range:

1. Select the cells or range you want to fill.

2. Enter the data or formula into the formula bar. Do not press Enter.

3. Press Ctrl+Enter to enter the data or formula into each of the selected cells.

Numbers or text appear as constant values in each of the selected cells. Formulas are filled into each selected cell as though they had been filled using **Edit Fill Right/Down** or **Edit Copy** and **Edit Paste**. Relative references in formulas adjust to their new locations.

## Turn on drag-and-drop to use powerful mouse techniques

 Many powerful mouse shortcuts are available when the drag-and-drop feature is turned on. Drag-and-drop enables you to move, copy, fill, or erase data or formulas quickly.

To turn on the drag-and-drop feature:

1. Choose the **Options Workspace** command.

2. Select the Cell **Drag** and Drop check box. This check box remains on until you turn it off by clearing it.

3. Choose OK or press Enter.

## Use drag-and-drop to move cells

When you use a mouse, a lot of shortcuts are available for rearranging your worksheet or macro sheet. One of these shortcuts enables you to move a cell or range by dragging it to a new location and dropping it.

To drag a cell or range to a new location:

1. Select a single cell or a range that is a single block.

2. Move the pointer to an edge of the selected cell or range. When the cell pointer is correctly positioned over an edge of the selection, the pointer changes from a cross to an arrowhead.

3. Hold down the mouse button and drag the cell or range to its new location. You see a shadowed outline of the cells being moved.

4. Release the mouse button to drop the cell or range at the new location.

Be careful that you do not position the pointer over the small square that appears at the lower right corner of a selection. This small square is used to fill cells by dragging.

## Use drag-and-drop to copy cells

You can use drag-and-drop also to copy a cell or range to a new location. When you copy formulas with drag-and-drop, you create copies the same as if you had used **Edit Copy** and **Edit Paste**. When you fill cells with drag-and-drop, relative cell references in formulas adjust to their new locations.

To drag-and-drop a copy:

1. Select a cell or a range that is a single block.

2. Move the pointer to an edge of the selected cell or range. When the cell pointer is correctly positioned over an edge of the selection, the pointer changes from a cross to an arrowhead.

3. Hold down the mouse button and the Ctrl key, then drag the shadowed outline to where you want the copy.

4. Release the mouse button and the Ctrl key.

(Notice that while you hold down the Ctrl key, a small plus sign appears next to the pointer, indicating that you can make a duplicate.)

## Drag the fill handle to fill cells with formulas or data

When the drag-and-drop feature is turned on, a small square appears at the lower right corner of the selected cell or range. By dragging this square, called the *fill handle*, you can fill data or formulas into adjacent cells.

To fill a formula or data into adjacent cells:

1. Select the cell or range containing the data or formula you want to copy.

2. Drag the fill handle in the direction you want filled. As you drag the handle, an outline surrounds the cells to be filled.

3. Release the mouse button to fill the cells.

Formulas are filled into cells as if you used Edit Fill Right/ Down. Relative references in formulas adjust as they would with other copy or fill operations. You can drag in any direction—up, down, left, or right, but you can fill in only one direction at a time.

## Use drag-and-drop to erase cells

Drag-and-drop can help you erase all or part of a range of cells. Make sure the drag-and-drop feature is on by choosing the Options Workspace command and selecting the Cell Drag and Drop check box, then choose OK.

To erase all or part of a range of cells:

1. Select the cells.

2. Drag the fill handle up or left. Cells below or to the right of the dragged area appear patterned.

3. Release the mouse button, and all the patterned cells are erased.

Figure 2.3 shows the direction to drag and the portions of the range erased when all months are selected and the fill handle is dragged to the left.

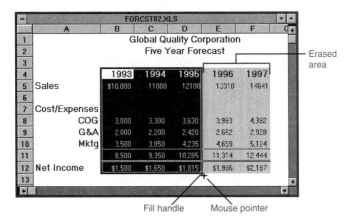

**Fig. 2.3**  *Drag the fill handle to the left to erase cells.*

If you want to completely erase a range using drag-and-drop, drag the fill handle up or left until the fill handle is over the top left cell in the original selection, then release the mouse button.

## Use Goto to return to one of the last four locations

Excel remembers the last four locations you moved to when you move using the Goto command or the F5 shortcut key. This capability enables you to go to a location, work there, then return to your original location.

To return to one of the last four locations:

1. Choose the Formula Goto command or press the F5 key.

2. The Goto dialog box appears, as shown in figure 2.4. The last four cells or ranges you selected with Goto appear at the top of the Goto list. Select one of these locations from the top of the list and choose OK, or double-click the location in the list.

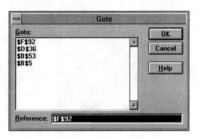

**Fig. 2.4** *The last four locations selected with Goto appear at the top of the list.*

## Use the Goto dialog box to select a large range

Selecting a large area by dragging across cells or using the Shift+arrow key combination is tedious. Instead, you can trick the Goto dialog box into making a large selection, as follows:

1. Select one corner of the large range.

2. Choose the Formula Goto command or press F5 to display the Goto dialog box.

3. In the Reference edit box, type the reference for the opposite corner or a cell close to the opposite corner.

4. Hold down the Shift key as you choose OK, or press Shift+Enter. This action selects the entire range from the original cell to the cell you typed.

If the cell you typed in step 3 is not the exact cell for the opposite corner, the range selected will not be the range you wanted. But you can adjust the current range. With the range still selected, use the scroll bars to scroll to where you can see the cell you want as the opposite corner. Hold down the Shift key as you click this new opposite corner. This action selects all the cells between the original cell and the new cell.

## Use Zoom to select one or more large areas

Excel's Zoom feature can make it easy to select one or more large areas. By reducing the size of the worksheet displayed in the window, you may be able to see and select all of the large area.

To reduce the worksheet so you can see more of it:

1.  Choose Window Zoom.

2.  The Zoom dialog box appears. Select 50% or 25% from the Magnification group, which gives you an *aerial view* of the worksheet.

3.  Choose OK.

4.  Click one corner of the area you want to select, then hold down the Shift key as you click the opposite corner. To select multiple areas, drag across the first area, then hold down the Ctrl key as you drag across each additional area.

To return to a normal-sized worksheet, choose Window Zoom, select 100%, then choose OK.

## Double-click to move the active cell across a block of cells

Excel has an express move that enables you to move the active cell quickly across a block of cells that are all filled or all empty. For this express technique to work, the drag-and-drop feature must be turned on. (For instructions, see "Turn on drag-and-drop to use powerful mouse techniques" earlier in this chapter.)

To move across a block of filled cells, double-click the edge of the active cell on the side you want to move. In figure 2.5, you would double-click the right edge of cell A8 to quickly move the active cell to cell F8. The mouse pointer changes to the arrowhead when it is correctly positioned over an edge, as it is in this figure. You can double-click any edge to make an express move in the direction of that side.

| | A | B | C | D | E | F | G |
|---|---|---|---|---|---|---|---|
| | | | FORCST02.XLS | | | | |
| 1 | | | Global Quality Corporation | | | | |
| 2 | | | Five Year Forecast | | | | |
| 3 | | | | | | | |
| 4 | | 1993 | 1994 | 1995 | 1996 | 1997 | |
| 5 | Sales | $10,000 | 11000 | 12100 | 13310 | 14641 | |
| 6 | | | | | | | |
| 7 | Cost/Expenses | | | | | | |
| 8 | COG | 3,000 | 3,300 | 3,630 | 3,993 | 4,392 | |
| 9 | G&A | 2,000 | 2,200 | 2,420 | 2,662 | 2,928 | |
| 10 | Mktg | 3,500 | 3,850 | 4,235 | 4,659 | 5,124 | |
| 11 | | 8,500 | 9,350 | 10,285 | 11,314 | 12,444 | |
| 12 | Net Income | $1,500 | $1,650 | $1,815 | $1,996 | $2,197 | |
| 13 | | | | | | | |

**Fig. 2.5**  *Double-click an edge to move quickly across cells.*

If you start with a filled cell as the active cell, the express action moves the active cell over contiguous filled cells until it reaches a blank cell. The selection stops on the last filled cell.

If you start with a blank cell as the active cell, the express action moves the active cell over contiguous blank cells until it reaches a filled cell. The active cell stops on the last blank cell.

## Use Shift+double-click to select blocks of cells

The express move using the double-click described in the preceding tip can be used to select the cells over which the active cell moves. To select cells as the active cell moves to its new location, hold down the Shift key as you double-click the edge of a cell.

## Use Ctrl+arrow to move or select across a long distance

Move across contiguous blocks of filled or empty cells by holding down the Ctrl key as you press the appropriate arrow key. For example, in figure 2.5, press Ctrl+right arrow to move the active cell right to cell F8.

If you start with the active cell on a filled cell, the active cell moves to the last filled cell in the direction of the arrow key you pressed. If you start with the active cell on a blank cell, the active cell moves to the last blank cell in the direction of the arrow key you pressed.

The express move using Ctrl+arrow can be used to also select the cells over which the active cell moves. To select cells as the active cell moves to its new location, hold down the Shift key as you press Ctrl+arrow key.

## Use Ctrl+Shift+* (asterisk) to select a block of cells

 Many times, you must select a large area of cells such as a database, a report to print, or data to chart. If you correctly design the block of data you want to select, the selection process is easy—you can do it with a keystroke combination. Selecting an entire block using the following procedure is also useful for recorded macros that must select a range that changes size.

In Excel, a *block* of cells is a group of cells that all touch on the edges or corners. This group of cells must be surrounded by the worksheet edge or blank cells. In effect, the block of cells must be an island unconnected to other parts of the worksheet. Other nondatabase cells do not touch the heading or data.

To select a block of cells with a single keystroke combination:

1. Select one cell in the block of cells that make up your database, report, or print area.

2. Press Ctrl+Shift+* (asterisk) to select a rectangular block that encloses all filled cells that touch. Use the asterisk on the typewriter keys, not on the numeric keypad.

After the block of cells is selected, you can give commands that affect blocks of data, such as Edit Clear, Edit Copy, Options Set Print Area, or any of the commands that affect selected cells.

You also can use Ctrl+Shift+* (asterisk) to select an area with the macro recorder. When you run the macro, Excel selects the range just as though you had pressed Ctrl+Shift+* (asterisk), even if the range has changed size or shape.

The Ctrl+Shift+* (asterisk) combination is a shortcut for choosing Formula Select Special and then selecting the Current Region option.

## Use Ctrl+drag to select separate blocks

If you must select more than one group of cells at a time, or select nontouching rows or columns, select the first cell, range, row, or column you want in the selection. Then hold down the Ctrl key as you select additional cells, ranges, rows, or columns. This action enables you to format all these areas with a single command.

**Note:** You cannot copy from multiple selections.

## Use Ctrl+Shift++ (plus sign) to insert cells, rows, or columns

Inserting cells, rows, or columns is often the easiest way to rearrange your worksheet or create a new working area on a worksheet. Inserting works by moving the selected cells, rows, or columns down or to the right. New blank cells, rows, or columns are inserted at the location of the original selection.

To insert new cells:

1. Select the cells where you want new blank cells inserted.

2. Press Ctrl+Shift++ (plus sign). Use the plus sign on the typing key.

3. The Insert dialog box appears. Select the direction you want existing cells to shift, then choose OK.

To insert new rows or columns:

1. Select the rows or columns where you want new rows or columns inserted. Select an entire row or column by clicking the row or column heading. With the keyboard, press Shift+spacebar to select the current row or press Ctrl+spacebar to select the current column.

2. Press Ctrl+Shift++ (plus sign). Use the plus sign on the typing key. The rows or columns are inserted immediately.

## Use Ctrl+- (hyphen) to delete cells, rows, or columns

Deleting cells, rows, or columns is different from clearing them. When you delete, you are pulling the cells, rows, or columns from the sheet as though they never existed. Cells, rows, or columns to the right or below move up or left to fill the vacuum that remains.

To delete cells:

1. Select the cells where you want existing cells deleted.

2. Press Ctrl+ - (hyphen). Use the hyphen on the typing key.

3. The Insert dialog box appears. Select the direction you want existing cells to shift to fill in the vacuum, then choose OK.

To delete entire rows or columns:

1. Select the rows or columns where you want rows or columns deleted.

2. Press Ctrl+ - (hyphen). Use the hyphen on the typing key. The rows or columns are deleted immediately.

## Use group edit to insert or delete through multiple worksheets

To insert or delete the same cells, rows, or columns in more than one worksheet, use Excel's group edit feature. When group edit is enabled, the changes to one worksheet are duplicated in other worksheets in the group.

To make the same insertion or deletion in multiple worksheets:

1. Open all worksheets you want to work with.

2. Activate the worksheet you want to make changes in. Other worksheets will reflect the changes you make to this worksheet.

3. Choose the Options Group Edit command.

4. Select from the Select Group list the worksheets you want to include in the group. To select a contiguous list of worksheets, click the topmost worksheet you want in the group, then hold down Shift as you click the lowest worksheet. To select a noncontiguous list of worksheets, click the first worksheet, then Ctrl+click the other worksheets you want in the group.

5. Choose OK or press Enter.

6. Insert or delete cells, rows, or columns through the active worksheet.

Changes you make to the active worksheet are made to other worksheets in the group. All worksheets in the group appear with [Group] in their titles. To get out of group mode, activate one of the other worksheets in the group.

## Use array formulas to protect a range against insertion or deletion

You may want to protect areas of your worksheet against the accidental insertion or deletion of rows or columns. For example, suppose that your calculations are in an area to the side of a formatted report. If you insert a row through the calculation area, you will probably affect the report's format.

Protecting the entire worksheet would prevent any insertions or deletions, but could also be inconvenient. Instead, protect a range of cells by entering an *array formula* along any side of an array you want to protect. Array formulas are a single formula entered into many cells.

Figure 2.6 shows the array formula = " " entered in cells
B5:B10 and cells C4:E4. These two sets of array formulas
protect the range C5:E10 against inserted or deleted rows
or columns. (The ranges B5:B10 and C4:E4 are outlined in
figure 2.6 only to make the range apparent, because this
formula results in a blank. Array formulas do not normally
have borders around their cells.)

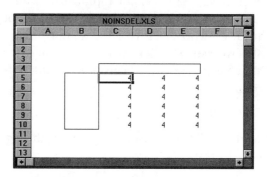

**Fig. 2.6**  *Enter an array formula along the sides of a range
to protect against accidental insertions or deletions.*

To enter an array formula:

1. Select the cells to contain the formula.

2. Enter the formula in the formula bar.

3. Press Ctrl+Shift+Enter.

To see the array formula, select any of the cells. Notice
that array formulas appear enclosed in braces, such as
{= " " }.

## Select cells by their content

Being able to select cells by their contents can be useful
for finding worksheet errors, values that should be formulas, and formulas that should be values.

To select cells containing a specific type of content:

1. Select a single cell if you want to find all the cells of a type throughout the worksheet. Select a range if you want to find all the cells of a type within a range.

2. Choose the Formula Select Special command. The Select Special dialog box appears (see fig. 2.7).

3. Select the Constants or Formulas option depending on whether you want the selection based on values entered in a cell or a formula's result.

4. Select one or more of the following check boxes:

| | |
|---|---|
| Numbers | Constant or formula result is a number |
| Text | Constant or formula result is text |
| Logicals | Constant or formula result is TRUE or FALSE |
| Errors | Constant or formula result is an Excel error, such as #DIV/0 |

5. Choose OK or press Enter. All the cells meeting the description you selected in steps 3 and 4 are selected.

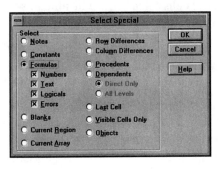

**Fig. 2.7**   *Use the Select Special dialog box to select cells with a specific content.*

The most common error in corporate worksheets is accidentally typing a number over a formula. If left unchecked, the results are incorrect because the number doesn't recalculate. To find this type of error, select a range containing what you think are only formulas, then use the Formula Select Special command with the Constants option and all check boxes selected. Any selected cells are constants and thus should not be in that area.

## Use Tab or Shift+Tab to move between cells in a selection

When you are checking formulas or errors in a worksheet, you may want to select an area and then check the contents of each cell in the area—without losing your selection.

For example, suppose that you use Formula Select Special to select cells containing errors. To see the formula causing an error, you must click the cell, thereby losing the selection of other cells that remain to be checked. There is a way, however, to move through contiguous or noncontiguous selections and check or edit each cell while retaining the selection.

To keep all the cells selected and be able to see the contents of each in the formula bar:

1. Press Tab or Shift+Tab to move between the cells until you find a cell you want to edit.

2. Press the F2 key or click the formula bar.

3. Edit the cell.

4. Press Tab or Shift+Tab to move to the next cell in the selection.

## Press Ctrl+. (period) to move to corners of a selection

When you select a large print area or database, you may not be able to see all the corners at one time. To move the active cell to each corner so you can see the corner on-screen, press Ctrl+. (period). Each time you press Ctrl+. (period), the active cell moves clockwise to the next corner.

## Use Ctrl+Backspace to display the active cell

Many times, the screen is scrolled so that you can no longer see the active cell. If you want to move the active cell back to the viewable portion of the window, press Ctrl+Backspace.

## Assign range names

 If you assign English-like names to areas of your worksheet, you can select areas easily. The areas even expand or contract if rows or columns are inserted or deleted through the original range. This means that the names still refer to the correct range even when you insert or delete cells, ranges, rows, or columns.

To assign an English-like name to a cell or range:

1. Select the cell or range of cells you want to refer to by name.

2. Choose the Formula Define Name command.

3. The Define Name dialog box appears. Select the Name edit box and type the name you will use to refer to the selected cell or range.

The name can contain letters, numbers, under-
scores, or periods, but cannot contain a space. You
can use up to 255 characters. Although some symbols can be used, many cannot, so you may find it
easiest to never use symbols.

4. Choose OK or press Enter.

5. If you want to preserve the name for the next time
   you open this file, save your worksheet or macro
   sheet.

Now that the name is assigned to this range, you can select the range by pressing F5 (the Goto key), selecting the
name from the list, and choosing OK. (Pressing F5 is the
same as choosing the Formula Goto command.)

## Use Views Manager to select and display areas

Use Excel's Views Manager when you must repeatedly
select a range of cells or set the same display or print settings. The Views Manager is one of the many add-ins that
come with Excel. If you did not install the Views Manager
during the initial installation, follow these steps:

1. Choose the Options Add-ins command.

2. The Add-In Manager dialog box appears. Choose the
   Add button.

3. The File Open dialog box appears. Select the
   VIEWS.XLA file from the EXCEL\LIBRARY directory
   and choose OK.

4. The Add-In Manager dialog box reappears and the
   words Views Manager appear in the list of available
   add-ins. Choose the Close button. The Window View
   command is now available whenever you run Excel.

If your computer does not have the LIBRARY directory or the VIEWS.XLA file, get your original Excel installation disks and start the Excel installation procedure. Use the Custom installation option. You do not need to reinstall all of Excel; install only the LIBRARY.

The Views Manager enables you to give an English-like name to selected cells, a window's display settings, and print settings. For example, you may have three views on a worksheet. In one view, you enter data with the gridlines on and the print area set for printing. In another view, you see the intermediary calculations. In the third view, you view and print the final results with the gridlines turned off.

To assign a name to a view:

1. Select the cells, then scroll the window until it appears as you want it to in the view. Select display settings with the **O**ptions **D**isplay command. If you want print settings remembered for this name, use the **O**ptions Set Print Area command and File Page Setup commands. Hide columns or rows you want hidden when this view appears.

2. Choose the **W**indow View command.

3. Choose the **A**dd button.

4. The Add View dialog box appears. Type the name for this view in the **N**ame edit box. If you want print settings saved with the name, select the **P**rint Settings check box. If you want hidden rows and columns displayed as you have set them, select the Hidden **R**ows & Columns check box.

5. Choose OK.

Your selections and settings are recorded with the name you typed. When you want to return to the view, choose the Window View command, select the name you want from the Views list, and choose the Show button. (If you do not see the Window View command, the Views Manager is not installed.)

# 3

# Using Toolbars

Toolbars are a major time-saver in Excel 4 because they enable you to quickly access commands you use frequently. The Excel toolbars can contain Excel tools and custom tools that you design. A few tools even hold hidden surprises.

## Use the shortcut menu to display the toolbar

If a toolbar is displayed in your worksheet, you can get to the toolbar commands easily. Click the displayed toolbar with the right mouse button. This action displays the Toolbar shortcut menu. Then click the name of the toolbar you want to display or hide.

## View a tool's description

Excel toolbars contain many tools, so it's easy to forget what they do. You can see what a tool does in two ways. Click and hold the mouse button on a tool. A description of the tool appears in the Status bar at the bottom of the screen. If you do not want to choose the tool's command, continue holding down the button, drag off the tool onto the worksheet, then release the mouse button.

If you want to browse through tool descriptions or want help on a tool, click the Help tool at the far right side of the standard toolbar. (The Help tool looks like an arrow pointer and a question mark.) After you click the Help tool, you can point to (but don't click) any tool on any toolbar and see its description in the Status bar at the bottom of the screen. If you click a tool, the Help window for that tool appears. Press the Esc key to return to a normal pointer.

## Shift+click a tool to get alternate commands

Some tools in the toolbar produce an alternate action if you hold down the Shift key as you click the tool. When you perform this action, the tool's face changes to reflect the Shift+click action.

If you are unsure of the action produced by holding the Shift key, you can see what the tool does by holding down the Shift key, putting the tip of the mouse pointer on the tool, and holding down the mouse button. Read the tool's description in the Status bar at the bottom of the screen. If you do not want to complete the tool's action, continue holding down the mouse button as you drag off the tool, then release the button.

You can free up room on a toolbar by learning the alternate tool actions, then deleting the tools that are the equivalent of alternate tool actions. Use the following table as a reference.

| Tool Face | Action | Shifted Tool Face | Shifted Action |
|-----------|--------|-------------------|----------------|

### Formatting and Editing

| Tool Face | Action | Shifted Tool Face | Shifted Action |
|-----------|--------|-------------------|----------------|
| | Paste formats | | Paste values |
| | Paste values | | Paste formats |
| | Increase font size | | Decrease font size |
| | Decrease font size | | Increase font size |
| | Format adds one decimal place | | Format removes one decimal place |
| | Format removes one decimal place | | Format adds one decimal place |
| | Delete selected cells | | Insert blank cells |
| | Insert blank cells | | Delete selected cells |
| | Delete selected rows | | Insert blank rows |
| | Insert blank rows | | Delete selected rows |
| | Delete selected columns | | Insert blank columns |
| | Insert blank columns | | Delete selected columns |

*continues*

| Tool Face | Action | Shifted Tool Face | Shifted Action |
|---|---|---|---|

**Printing and Document Management**

| | | | |
|---|---|---|---|
|  | Print document |  | Preview document |
|  | Preview document |  | Print document |
|  | Increase document magnification |  | Decrease document magnification |
|  | Decrease document magnification |  | Increase document magnification |
|  | Sort ascending order |  | Sort descending order |
|  | Sort descending order |  | Sort ascending order |
|  | Promote selected rows |  | Demote selected rows |
|  | Demote selected rows |  | Promote selected rows |

**Drawing**

| | | | |
|---|---|---|---|
|  | Draw empty rectangle |  | Draw filled rectangle |
|  | Draw filled rectangle |  | Draw empty rectangle |
|  | Draw empty oval |  | Draw filled oval |
|  | Draw filled oval |  | Draw empty oval |

| Tool Face | Action | Shifted Tool Face | Shifted Action |
|---|---|---|---|
| | Draw empty arc | | Draw filled arc |
| | Draw filled arc | | Draw empty arc |
| | Draw empty polygon | | Draw filled polygon |
| | Draw filled polygon | | Draw empty polygon |
| | Draw empty freehand | | Draw filled freehand |
| | Draw filled freehand | | Draw empty freehand |
| | Group objects | | Ungroup objects |
| | Ungroup objects | | Group objects |
| | Bring object to front | | Send object to back |
| | Send object to back | | Bring object to front |

**Macros**

| Tool Face | Action | Shifted Tool Face | Shifted Action |
|---|---|---|---|
| | Run macro | | Step macro |
| | Step macro | | Run macro |

## Change the toolbar

Many more tools are available than those shown in the
default Excel toolbars. You can add, remove, rearrange,

or move tools. You can even drag tools from one toolbar to another. First, though, you must access the Customize dialog box:

1. Display all the toolbars you want to modify.

2. Choose Options Toolbars to display the Toolbars dialog box (see fig. 3.1).

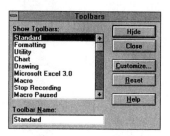

**Fig. 3.1** *Add, hide, or restore toolbars from the Toolbars dialog box.*

3. Select the Customize button from the Toolbars dialog box. The Customize dialog box appears, as shown in figure 3.2.

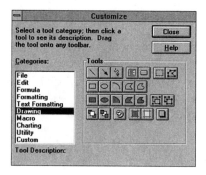

**Fig. 3.2** *Modify any toolbar while the Customize dialog box is displayed.*

Each category in the dialog box contains groups of tools. The tool faces are shown in the Tools group on the right side of the dialog box. If you are unfamiliar with a tool face, click and hold the face and you will see a description of the tool's action at the bottom of the dialog box.

Follow these steps to add a tool:

1. Make sure that the Customize dialog box is displayed.

2. Select the tool collection containing the type of tool you want from the Categories list.

3. Drag the tool face from the Tools group to the toolbar. Release the tool where you want it to appear in the toolbar.

4. Repeat steps 2 and 3 until the tools you want are added to the toolbars.

5. Choose the Close button.

To remove a tool from the toolbar, make sure that the Customize dialog box is displayed. Next, drag the tool off the toolbar and onto the worksheet, then release the tool.

Other ways to change the toolbar follow:

| | |
|---|---|
| Rearrange | In the same toolbar drag the tool, then drop it. |
| Insert spaces | Drag the tool one half tool width to the right, then drop it. |
| Delete | Drag the tool off the toolbar onto a worksheet or blank area, then drop it. |
| Move | Drag the tool from one toolbar to its new location on another toolbar. |

| Copy | Hold down Ctrl, then drag the tool from one toolbar to another location on the same toolbar or to a different toolbar. |

## Create custom toolbars

 You can create your own toolbar. To do so, begin by displaying the Toolbars dialog box (refer to fig. 3.1). In the Toolbar Name edit box, type the name of the toolbar you want to add, then choose the Add button. The Customize dialog box (refer to fig. 3.2) appears. While the Customize dialog box is displayed, you can drag tools from the Tools group and drop them in your custom toolbar. (Your custom toolbar is available in Excel until you delete it.)

## Press Ctrl+7 to display or hide the standard toolbar

Press Ctrl+7 to display or hide the standard toolbar. Each press toggles the standard toolbar on or off. Make sure that you press Ctrl+7, not Ctrl+F7. (Use the 7 on the typing keyboard, not on the numeric pad.)

## Click the close icon to close a floating toolbar

To quickly close toolbars in a floating palette, click the close icon in the toolbar. The close icon appears as a small dash at the top left corner of unattached toolbars.

## Control the chart toolbar

The way the chart toolbar seems to appear and disappear can be confusing. Normally, the chart toolbar appears when a chart is active and disappears when a worksheet is active. This rule is broken, however, if you show or hide the chart toolbar manually:

- To hide the chart toolbar so that it does not appear when a chart is displayed, hide the toolbar while the chart is active.

- To display the chart toolbar at all times, activate a worksheet and then display the chart toolbar.

- To hide the chart toolbar at all times, activate a chart and then hide the chart toolbar.

To show or hide a toolbar:

1. Choose the **O**ptions **T**oolbars command.

2. Select the toolbar from the Show Toolbars list.

3. Select the **S**how or H**i**de button as appropriate. The **S**how and H**i**de button are the same button. The button's label changes depending on which command is appropriate for the toolbar you selected.

## Reset or delete a toolbar

Reduce the clutter of unwanted or changed toolbars by resetting built-in toolbars to their original order. When you are finished using a custom toolbar, you can delete it.

To reset a built-in toolbar:

1. Choose the **O**ptions **T**oolbars command.

2. In the Toolbars dialog box, select the toolbar you want to restore.

3. Select the **R**eset button.

To delete a custom toolbar:

1. Choose the **Options Toolbars** command.

2. In the Toolbars dialog box, select the toolbar you want to delete.

3. Select the **Delete** button. Be careful when you delete a toolbar because you cannot undo the deletion.

## Draw your own tool

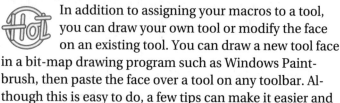
In addition to assigning your macros to a tool, you can draw your own tool or modify the face on an existing tool. You can draw a new tool face in a bit-map drawing program such as Windows Paintbrush, then paste the face over a tool on any toolbar. Although this is easy to do, a few tips can make it easier and give you better results.

To create a custom tool face:

1. Display the Customize dialog box by choosing the **Options Toolbars** command and then choosing the Customize button. (Fig. 3.2 shows the Customize dialog box.) The Customize dialog box must be displayed while you copy tool faces, paste tool faces, or modify tools.

2. Press Ctrl+Esc and switch to the Program Manager. Start the Windows Paintbrush application or any other bit-map drawing program.

3. Draw a tool face.

4. Select your drawing, then copy it to the Clipboard. (If you are using Paintbrush, select your drawing with the rectangular selection tool.)

5. Press Ctrl+Esc and activate Excel.

6. With the Customize dialog box displayed, click the tool you want to paste a new face on, then choose the Edit Paste Tool Face command.

7. Close the Customize dialog box.

## Modify the face on a tool

You can change the face of a tool on a predefined toolbar or a custom tool. To change a tool face:

1. Display the toolbar containing the tool with the face you want to change.

2. Display the Customize dialog box as described previously.

3. Click the tool you want to change, then choose Edit Copy Tool Face. (This command is available only when the Customize dialog box is displayed.)

4. Switch to the Program Manager by pressing Ctrl+Esc.

5. Start Windows Paintbrush, which can be found in the Accessories group.

6. Choose the Edit Paste command to paste the tool face.

7. Before you click anywhere in the background, drag the tool face to the middle of the screen. This gives you room to work on all sides of the face.

8. The tool face will be too small to edit accurately, so choose View Zoom In. You can use the colors and the paintbrush tools to edit the individual dots in the tool face. When you are finished, choose View Zoom Out to return to the normal screen. Use the rectangular selection tool to copy the same size tool face as the original you pasted.

9. Press Ctrl+Esc and switch to Excel.

10. With the Customize dialog box still displayed, click the tool you want to receive the new face, then choose Edit Paste Tool Face. You can paste a new face over a tool in a toolbar, but not over a tool in the various Categories in the Customize dialog box.

## Use the blank tool face as a template for custom tool faces

If you draw a custom tool face that is too large, Excel compresses it to fit when it pastes the tool—this distorts your wonderful artwork. To make it easy to get the right size tool, select Custom from the Categories list in the Customize dialog box. One of the Custom tool faces is blank. If you copy it into Paintbrush, you will have a square of the right size for your tool face's background.

## Save and transfer customized toolbars

When you quit Excel, the current toolbars and tools are stored in the EXCEL.XLB file in the WINDOWS directory. You can save a collection of toolbars for later use or to give to another Excel user.

To save a collection of toolbars that you have modified:

1. Exit Excel.

2. Use the File Manager to copy EXCEL.XLB to *special*.XLB, where *special* is the new name (such as FINANCE.XLB). You can have many XLB files saved with different names.

When you want to use one of these toolbar collections:

1. Exit Excel.

2. If you want to keep your original toolbars, rename the EXCEL.XLB file to EXCEL.BAK or a similar name. Then you can rename it as EXCEL.XLB when you want to return to the original collection of toolbars.

3. Use the File Copy command to copy your *special*.XLB over EXCEL.XLB.

4. Restart Excel.

To transfer your collection of toolbars to other Excel users:

1. If the other users want to keep their original toolbars, rename their EXCEL.XLB file to EXCEL.BAK or a similar name. In this way, it can be renamed as EXCEL.XLB when they want to return to their original collection of toolbars.

2. Use the File Copy command to copy your EXCEL.XLB file over their EXCEL.XLB file.

3. Start Excel to see the new collection of toolbars.

## Run Solitaire from the toolbar

That most insidious time-waster, Solitaire, can be instantly available from the Excel toolbar. To start Solitaire from a toolbar, you must first add the Card Pack tool:

1. Display the Customize dialog box as described previously, and choose Custom from the Categories list.

2. The Card Pack is at the right side of the top row of the Custom tools group. Drag the Card Pack to a toolbar, then drop it.

3. The Assign to Tool dialog box appears. Do *not* click a macro name. Instead, choose Cancel.

4. The Customize dialog box reappears. Choose Close.

This leaves you with the Card Pack tool on the toolbar, but no macro assigned to it. To start Solitaire, click the Card Pack tool. Solitaire activates over Excel. To return to Excel, press Alt+Tab.

## Display secret animation and a list of developers

On most personal computers, you can display an animated skit and the names of the people who developed Excel with the following trick. Sometimes, the animation runs only once, and you must repeat the entire process to see it again.

To see the names of the Excel developers and an animated display:

1. Add a new Card Pack tool to the standard toolbar using the technique described in the preceding tip.

2. Choose Cancel in the Assign to Tool dialog box so you do not assign a macro to the tool.

3. Close the Customize dialog box.

4. To activate the animation, hold down the Shift, Ctrl, and Alt keys while you click the Card Pack tool.

You will see the animation followed by a list of the members of the development team.

# 4

# Entering, Checking, and Protecting Data

After you build your worksheet, you must perform the mundane task of entering data. Excel has many ways to make entering data easier and faster, whether the data consists of numbers, dates, or text.

## Use shortcut keys to enter the current date and time

To enter the current date in a cell, press Ctrl+; (semi-colon). This action enters the day portion (integer) of the date-time serial number. Excel uses the date from your computer's internal clock. The date is automatically formatted with the standard date format.

To enter the current time in a cell, press Ctrl+Shift+: (colon). This action enters the time portion (decimal fraction) of the date-time serial number. Excel uses the time from your computer's internal clock. The time is automatically formatted with the standard time format.

If you want to change the format Excel uses as the standard date and time format, open the Control Panel in the Main group of the Program Manager. Start the International application. In the International dialog box, use the Date Format and Time Format groups to change the default date-time format.

## Copy the value from the cell above

If you are working in a database or with a column of entries, you can save time by not retyping entries that are the same as the contents of the cell above. To copy only the value (not the formula) from the cell above, press Ctrl+Shift+" (quotation mark).

## Use Ctrl+Enter to put one entry in multiple cells

You can quickly enter a number, a date, text, or a formula into more than one cell with the following technique:

1. Select all the cells in which you want to enter the number, date, text, or formula. The cells do not have to be adjacent.

2. Type the number, date, text, or formula into the formula bar.

3. Press Ctrl+Enter.

The result is the same as if you made the entry in one cell and then used Edit Copy and Edit Paste to make copies to the other cells. Relative references in formulas adjust to their new locations just as if they were copied and pasted. Be careful not to press Ctrl+Shift+Enter, a similar keystroke used for array formulas.

## Use group edit to put entries in multiple worksheets

When the group edit option is on, the data you enter in one worksheet is entered in the same location in other worksheets in the group. To use group edit:

1. Open or unhide all the worksheets in which you want to enter data. Activate the worksheet in which you want to work.

2. Choose the Options Group Edit command.

3. In the Group Edit dialog box that appears, select the worksheets in which you want your entries reflected. To select more than one worksheet, click one worksheet then use Ctrl+click to select additional worksheets.

4. Choose OK. [Group] is appended to each worksheet's name to indicate that you are in group edit mode.

5. Enter your data. It passes through to the same cells in other worksheets in the group.

When you finish entering data, exit the group edit mode by activating any other worksheet.

## Download data rather than retype it

You can avoid hours of work by saving data to disk in a format that Excel can read rather than retyping data from printed reports. Most personal computer, minicomputer, and mainframe applications can convert their data to a disk file in dBASE III, dBASE IV, Lotus 1-2-3, or text format.

Excel can read these files and separate the data into worksheet cells. In Excel 3 and Excel 4, text files are read most easily in a comma-separated value (CSV) format. This format separates all cells of data with commas. Any data that contains a comma, such as currency or a city-state combination, is enclosed in quotation marks. If you use CSV format, change the file extension to CSV and read the file into Excel. Most CSV files can be created with a mainframe report writer and a few hours work. After the report writer generates the report format, it can be used for all your CVS file conversions of the same data.

Excel 4 can read into a new worksheet a text file in which the fields (columns or cells) of data are separated by characters other than the comma used in CSV files. Excel 4 automatically reads and separates text files in which the fields of data are separated by a character other than a comma. To read a file using a different separator:

1. Choose File **O**pen. Choose the Text button to display the Text File Options dialog box (see fig. 4.1).

**Fig. 4.1**  *Excel can parse files with many types of column separators.*

2. Select from the Column Delimiter group the type of character that separates each field of data. If there is not a check box for the character used in your data, select Custom and type the character in the Custom edit box.

3. Select from the File Origin group the type of character set used to create the data file. Choose OK to return to the Open dialog box.

4. Select the file you want to open and choose OK.

## Use Paste Special to change numbers entered as text to numeric values

Files from other personal computer applications or downloaded from mainframe applications may have numbers entered as text. This may occur because of formatting limitations in applications such as Lotus 1-2-3 or an incorrectly written report generator from a mainframe. (A number entered as text is preceded by an apostrophe.)

Some functions in Excel may be unable to coerce numbers entered as text to numeric values, and math or worksheet errors will result. To change these text-numbers to numeric values:

1. Type **0** (zero) into a cell and copy that cell using **Edit Copy**. Select all the cells containing text-numbers.

2. Choose the **Edit Paste Special** command to display the Paste Special dialog box.

3. Select the Paste **Values** option and the Operation **Add** option. Choose OK.

This adds zero to all cells. The values in the cells don't change, but the text-numbers are forced to become numeric values so the addition will work. If you do this conversion frequently, you may want to record it as a macro.

## Use Formula Replace to convert text-numbers preceded by a quotation mark or caret

If your text-numbers are preceded by a quotation mark (") or a caret (^), you can convert them with a technique other than Paste Special as follows:

1. Select all the cells containing text-numbers. Choose the **Formula Replace** command.

2. In the Find What edit box, type the character you want removed (for example, the quotation mark). In the Replace With edit box, don't type anything. This combination removes the character preceding the number.

You may want to use Find Next and Replace to test how it works. After you are satisfied it works correctly, choose the Replace All command.

## Enter part numbers or phone numbers as text

Excel's automatic formatting of numbers is usually a time-saver, but can get in the way if you want to enter numbers as text, such as a part number or a telephone number. For example, your company may use part numbers such as

08597A
019875
005678

The problem with this type of number is that Excel strips the leading zeros from numbers that do not contain a text character. One solution is to format the entry cells with a custom numeric format, such as 000000. This action ensures that there will be a zero as a placeholder for every digit. Formatting a range with a custom numeric format is an easy way to work with leading zeros when you must enter them in a large range of cells. To create a custom numeric format:

1. Choose the Format Number command. The Number Format dialog box appears.

2. Type the custom format, **000000**, in the Code edit box. Choose OK or press Enter.

You can re-use this custom numeric format on this worksheet without re-creating it. It will appear at the bottom of the Format Codes list. In Excel 4, another and perhaps simpler method is to type an apostrophe (') before each number you want treated as text. The apostrophe indicates to Excel 4 to treat the number as text. Excel aligns the number as text and doesn't use numeric formatting on it, preserving the leading zeros.

## Use drag-and-drop to create date series

The drag-and-drop feature of Excel 4 can extend date series like those shown in figure 4.2. If you need to create a series of text labels indicating quarters of a year, type **Q1**, **Qtr 1**, or **Quarter 1** into the first cell in the series. Select that cell and drag the fill handle as many cells as you need filled with labels, then release the mouse button. As row 4 in figure 4.2 shows, Excel understands you are filling in quarters and automatically repeats the series after the fourth quarter. (The row above each formatted row displays how labels were entered before being converted to a date series.)

Suppose that you need a series of sequential dates like the date series in row 8 in figure 4.2. Type in the first date (called the *seed date*) in the leftmost cell, drag the fill handle for as many cells as you need filled with dates, then release the mouse button. The date is automatically incremented by one day per cell.

If you need a series of dates that all fall on the same day of the month, type in the first two dates, for example, **11-Oct-93** and **11-Nov-93**, then select both dates and drag to the right. Notice in row 12 how the dates automatically increment by one month, the difference between 10/11/93 and 11/11/93. If the calculated date from the series is greater than the last day in a month, drag-and-drop enters the last day of that month. If you don't see the fill handle in the lower right corner of the selected cell, choose Options Workspace and the Cell Drag and Drop check box, then choose OK.

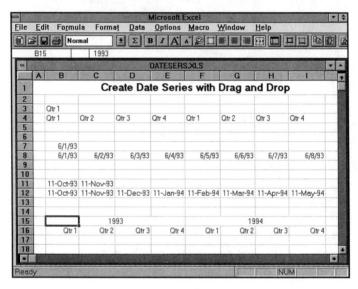

**Fig. 4.2**  *Use drag-and-drop to enter a series of dates.*

## Use the fill handle to enter a series of sequential text

To enter a series containing a combination of text and numbers (for example, Product 6, Flight 405, Item 512), the numbers must be at the end of the text. Enter the first text label and follow it with the first number in the series. The text label and number can be separated by one or more spaces. Select the cell containing this entry and drag the fill handle to the right or down. The cells you drag across fill with the same text label followed by the next number in the sequence (for example, Product 7, Product 8, Product 9, and so on). If you don't see the fill handle in the lower right corner of the selected cell, choose Options Workspace and the Cell Drag and Drop check box, then choose OK.

## Use drag-and-drop to enter a series of titles

The series of year and quarter labels shown in figure 4.2 can be useful in many business reports. With Excel 4 you can create headings quickly, without retyping quarter titles or years. To create the first year's titles:

1. Turn on drag-and-drop by choosing Options Workspace and the Cell Drag and Drop check box.

2. Select a cell and enter one of the types of quarter titles Excel 4 recognizes: **Q1**, **Qtr 1**, or **Quarter 1**.

3. Select this cell and drag it right three more cells. Release the mouse button and Excel enters the titles for quarters 2, 3, and 4.

4. Select the cell above the first quarter and enter the year. (In figure 4.2, the year is entered in cell B15.)

5. Select the cell containing the year and the three cells to the right, which are above the other quarter titles. To center the year title, you can click the Center In Selection tool on the Standard toolbar, or you can choose the Format Alignment command, then the Center across Selection option, then OK.

   This creates a block of cells two rows high by four columns wide containing the first year and quarters. Your worksheet should now look like cells B15:E16 in figure 4.2.

6. Select cells B15:E16 and drag the fill handle to the right across a set of four cells for every year. (If you

want to include two more years, for example, drag across eight cells.) Release the mouse button when you have selected as many cells as you need.

The first two-by-four block of cells (B15:E16) is repeated across the selection. But every four cells, the year is increased by one and the four quarters are repeated.

## Use glossaries to enter repetitive data

If you frequently enter long titles, formulas, numbers, phrases, or descriptions, you can use the Edit Glossary command, which is an add-in feature of Excel. The glossary enables you to store long text or numbers and enter them by typing an abbreviation. Glossaries can ensure that descriptions or phrases are typed correctly. The Excel glossary is similar to the Glossary command in word processors such as Word for Windows. To use the glossary feature, you must first install the Glossary add-in as follows:

1. Choose the Options Add-ins command.

2. From the Add-In Manager dialog box that appears, choose the Add button.

3. From the File Open dialog box that appears, select the GLOSSARY.XLA file, which is usually found in the EXCEL\LIBRARY directory.

4. When the Add-In Manager dialog box returns, choose the Close button, unless you want to include other add-ins.

The glossary command is now available whenever you run Excel. To remove the glossary add-in, reopen the Add-In Manager, select the Worksheet Glossary add-in from the list, and choose the Remove button. To add to the glossary:

1. Type the text, formula, or number into a cell or range of cells and select all the cells you want stored under a single abbreviation in the glossary.

2. Choose the Edit Glossary command, which displays the dialog box in figure 4.3.

3. In the Name edit box, type an abbreviation that identifies this entry.

4. Choose the Define button to add the contents of the cell or range to the glossary.

5. When the dialog reappears, you can define more entries or choose the Close button.

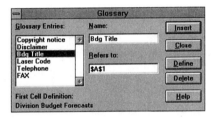

**Fig. 4.3** *Use the Edit Glossary add-in command to save retyping of frequent entries.*

To enter an item stored in the glossary:

1. Select the cell in which you want the entry. Choose the Edit Glossary command.

2. Select the abbreviation for the text you want from the Glossary Entries list. The first portion of the glossary entry you selected appears at the bottom of the dialog box. Choose Insert.

## Use Character Map or ANSI codes to enter special characters

With Excel you aren't limited to the characters you see on the keycaps of your keyboard. You can use all the characters in your Windows font sets. Some nonkeyboard characters that you may find useful are the copyright, trademark, registered, Japanese yen, English pound, and degree symbols.

In Excel 4, you can enter special characters using the Character Map in the Accessories program window. In Excel 3 or Excel 4, you can type the ANSI code using a special key combination. Using the Character Map accessory is the easiest way to enter a special character if you do it infrequently or if you are unsure of the available characters in the font you are using.

To find special characters in the Character Map and use them in a worksheet:

1. Switch to the Program Manager, open the Accessories group window, and start the Character Map application. Figure 4.4 shows the Character Map with the characters for the True Type font Wingdings.

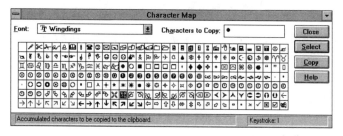

**Fig. 4.4** *Use the Character Map to select special characters for use in Excel.*

2. Select the font you want to use from the Font pull-down list. Usually, you should use the same font as the one used in similar parts of the worksheet. If the special character is not available in that font, check another font.

3. Select the special character you want by clicking it or by pressing the arrow keys. Notice that when you select a character, it magnifies so you can see the character in more detail.

4. Choose the **S**elect button to transfer your selected character to the Characters to Copy edit box. You can transfer more than one character into this edit box.

5. When all the characters you want are in the Characters to Copy edit box, choose the **C**opy button, then close the Character Map by choosing the Close button or pressing Esc.

6. Return to Excel by pressing Ctrl+Esc, selecting Excel, and choosing the **S**witch to button.

7. Select the worksheet cell where you want the character to appear and choose the Edit **P**aste command. The characters you selected appear in the cell.

When you select a character in the Character Map, its ANSI code appears in the lower right corner of the Character Map window. You can use this four-digit code to enter the character directly in Excel 3 or Excel 4. Some common characters and their ANSI character codes for the Times New Roman and Arial fonts follow:

| Special Character | Name | Key Combination (Numeric Keypad) |
| --- | --- | --- |
| ™ | Trademark symbol | Alt+0153 |
| ® | Registration mark | Alt+0174 |
| © | Copyright symbol | Alt+0169 |
| § | Legal section mark | Alt+0167 |
| ¢ | Cent mark | Alt+0162 |
| £ | English pound | Alt+0163 |
| ¥ | Japanese yen | Alt+0165 |

All the characters in the cell must be the same font as the special character you want to enter. The Alt+#### combinations must be entered using the numeric keypad. If the numeric keypad acts like arrow keys, press the NumLock key once to switch the numeric keypad from arrow keys to number keys. (On most keyboards, a lighted indicator shows when NumLock is on.)

To type 24¢ in a cell, for example, you would type **24**, then hold down the Alt key as you type **0162** (the character's four-digit numeric code). When you release the Alt key, the special character appears in the formula bar. You would continue typing if you wanted more characters to follow the special character.

## Use the Word for Windows 2 Equation Editor to create graphic objects for equations

You may need to reproduce scientific, engineering, or statistical equations on the worksheet. If you use Excel 4 and Word for Windows 2 or greater, you can use the Equation Editor in Word for Windows to embed a graphical object showing the equation or any math symbol. This embedded object is only a picture and cannot calculate results. You can format it as you would any graphical object.

Figure 4.5 shows the Equation Editor. An equation you create in the Equation Editor is embedded in your worksheet as an OLE object, and can be edited by double-clicking it.

To embed an equation in your Excel 4 worksheet:

1. Click the cell in which you want the top left corner of the equation.

2. Choose the Edit Insert Object command.

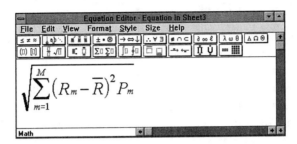

**Fig. 4.5** *Embed equations into your worksheet.*

3. Select Equation from the Object Type list and choose OK.

4. Create your equation by selecting symbols and inserting them in the equation window. Use the Help menu to learn more about the Equation Editor.

5. When you complete your equation, choose File Exit and Return. A dialog asks whether you want to save changes to your worksheet. Choose Yes.

The equation you create appears as a graphical object in your Excel 4 worksheet. You can size, format, and position it as you would any graphical object. As long as the Equation Editor is on the same personal computer as Excel 4, you can edit the equation by double-clicking it.

## Use the dictionary to check the spelling in your worksheet

Excel 4 contains a dictionary that checks text in cells that do not contain formulas. To check the spelling of text in your worksheet, select the range you want to check, then choose the Options Spelling command. If you use Word for Windows 2.0 or higher, Excel and Word share the same dictionary. Words you add to the dictionary in one of these programs are used when checking spelling in the other application.

## Add custom dictionaries to Excel

Excel and Word for Windows can use the same custom dictionaries. (They always use the same main spelling dictionary.) To use a custom dictionary with your worksheet, select it from the Add Words To pull-down list in the Spelling dialog box. Word for Windows and Excel custom dictionaries are stored under the WINDOWS directory in the \WINDOWS\MSAPPS\PROOF path.

As you spell check a worksheet or Word document, choose the Add button to add unrecognized words to the custom dictionary named in the Add Words To pull-down list. You can create new custom dictionaries for different kinds of work by typing in a new dictionary name in the Add Words To edit box. The name of your custom dictionary must end with the DIC extension, for example, FINANCL.DIC, TECH.DIC, ACRONYM.DIC, ABBREV.DIC, or GOVT.DIC. The words stored in each DIC file must be in alphabetical order for the Suggest portion of spell to work correctly.

## Use a text editor to add groups of words to the dictionary

You do not have to add words to a custom dictionary one at a time through the Spelling dialog box. Instead, you can edit an existing dictionary by using a text editor (such as the Notepad in the Windows Accessories group) or a word processor (such as Word for Windows) that works with text files. If you want to create a new custom dictionary, begin with a blank document and follow the next steps from step 2.

1. Change to the \WINDOWS\MSAPPS\PROOF directory and open the custom dictionary file you want to edit. You may need to change the file name pattern to *.DIC and press Enter to see a listing of existing

dictionary files. If you open a custom dictionary in a word processor, rather than a text editor, you may be asked to identify that it is a text file. Figure 4.6 shows a custom dictionary open in Notepad, which is the text editor that comes with Windows.

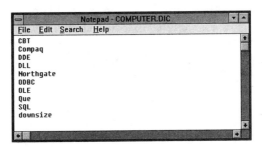

**Fig. 4.6** *Use the Notepad to edit or enhance your custom dictionary.*

2. Edit, delete, or add words to the list. The words you see will be used as the valid spelling list after the main (predefined) spell check is complete. You may want someone to check a printout of your list before you use or distribute it.

3. Sort the list in ascending alphabetical order. You must manually cut (Ctrl+X) and paste (Ctrl+V) to move words in Notepad. If you are using a word processor, use its sort feature. To sort in Word for Windows, for example, select the entire document, then choose the Tools Sorting command. When the Sorting dialog box appears, choose OK to accept the default settings.

4. If you are using a word processor, change the file format to Text. In Word for Windows, choose the File Save As command, then select Text Only (*.TXT) from the Save File as Type pull-down list.

5. Name the file with a recognizable file name and use the .DIC file extension.

6. Change to the \WINDOWS\MSAPPS\PROOF directory if that is not already the current directory, then choose OK or press Enter.

You can follow this procedure also to delete or correct a word you add accidentally to a custom dictionary. If you want to delete a custom dictionary, not just a word, delete the appropriate .DIC file from the directory \WINDOWS\MSAPPS\PROOF.

## Check a word in a formula by selecting the cell

Excel does not check the spelling of words in cells that contain a formula. If you want to check the spelling of a word that is in a formula, select the cell so that the formula appears in the formula bar. Select the word or words you want to check, then choose the **O**ptions **S**pelling command.

## Freeze formulas to preserve their values

You may want to freeze a formula so that its result does not change. This replaces the cell's formula with the value of the formula's result. To freeze a formula in a cell or formulas in a range of cells:

1. Select the cell or range of cells. Choose Edit Copy.

2. Keep the same selection and choose the Edit Paste **S**pecial command.

3. Select Paste Values and Operation None. Choose OK or press Enter. This pastes the values in the original selection over the formulas.

## Use the NOW function to display the current date and time

 If you want your worksheet or report to show the current date and time, enter =NOW() in the appropriate cell. This function returns the date and time from your computer's clock every time the worksheet recalculates. If you want to force it to update, press F9, the Calculate key. If you want to freeze the date and time so that it doesn't change, use the method described in the preceding tip, "Freeze formulas to preserve their values."

Use the Format Number command to format the cell with the date or time format you need. If you enter a date in a column that is narrow due to other report formatting, the date or time may not display. In a cell that is too narrow, the date or time appears as ####. If the date or time will not display because the cell is not wide enough, use the formula =TEXT(NOW(),"mmm d, yy"). This formula converts the date/time serial number returned by NOW to text using the format described by "mmm d, yy". You can put any predefined or custom numeric format in the quotation marks to get the date and time format you want. Because the date or time is text, it can extend beyond cell boundaries and can be formatted with the methods you use to format any text. The date or time continues to update when the worksheet recalculates.

## Use custom range formats to check data entry

Excel 4 can format numbers differently depending on the value of the number. You can use this capability as a simple but effective method of checking that values are in a correct range. For example, if valid numbers are between 500 and 1000 and the user types the number 450, you could display the number in red and show the text message `Too low`. If the number is higher than 1000, you might display the number in blue and include the text message `Too high`. To create a custom numeric format that changes the appearance of the entry depending on the value:

1.  Select the cells you want to format. Choose Format Number.

2.  In the Code edit box, type a custom format like the ones described in the following paragraphs. Choose OK.

Create a code by entering a conditional operator in square brackets in the Code edit box. If the number in a cell satisfies the condition, that portion of the custom format is used. The conditionals are the same as those used in formulas: <, <=, =, =>, and >.

For example, the custom format

```
[Blue][>1000]0.00;[Red][<500]0.00;[Black]0.00
```

formats numbers greater than 1000 as blue, numbers less than 500 as red, and all numbers in between as black. In this example, all numbers use the numeric format 0.00.

In the following example, a text message and the number appear in color:

```
[Blue][>1000]0.00 "Too high";[Red][<500]0.00
  "Too low";[Black]0.00
```

The column containing the number must be wide enough to show the number and text. Otherwise, the cell will fill with as many # symbols as necessary to fill the cell width. You can show only text when a number is typed by removing the number format (0.00) and including only the quoted text for that portion of the format.

## Use the IF function to check numeric ranges

Use the IF function to display a text warning if a numeric entry is out of range. For example, you can type the following formula in cell D6 to check the entry in cell C6:

```
=IF(C6<10,"Below 10",IF(C6>20,"Above 20",""))
```

This formula first checks if C6 is less than 10; if it is, Below 10 appears in cell D6. If the entry in C6 is greater than or equal to 10, the second IF function works. The second IF function displays Above 20 when the number in C6 is greater than 20. If the number is 10 to 20, the quotation marks at the end of the formula display nothing. (If you leave out the quotation marks at the end of the formula, the word FALSE appears when the number is 10 to 20.)

## Use IF, AND, and DATEVALUE to check date ranges

You can check for valid date entries using the IF, AND, and DATEVALUE functions. In the following example, you type the date in cell C8 using any of the date formats that Excel recognizes. The formula can be entered in any other cell, but you will probably want it near the entry cell so you can see whether the entry is valid.

```
=IF(AND(C8>DATEVALUE("1/31/93"),C8<DATEVALUE
("3/1/93")),"", "Incorrect date")
```

The formula checks to see whether the date in C8 is both greater than 1/31/93 and less than 3/1/93. This means valid dates must be in the month of February 1993. Typing a February 1993 date in C8 results in "", which displays nothing in the cell containing the formula. When an invalid date is typed, the text Incorrect date appears.

If you want to be able to type the upper and lower date limits into cells so that the limits can be changed more easily, use

```
=IF(AND(C8>M90,C8<N90),"","Incorrect date")
```

In this example, M90 contains the lower date limit and N90 contains the upper date limit. You can type the dates into the cells using any date format that Excel recognizes.

## Build a table to store limits for data checking

Although the previous formulas are easy to use, they can be difficult to review and maintain if data entry limits change. Each formula must be checked and edited if the upper or lower limits change.

A better approach is to put all the upper and lower limits in one area of the worksheet. You might call this area a data checking table. In the following example, a data checking table holds all the upper and lower numeric and date limits for all checks in the worksheet.

```
=IF(AND(C11>G52,C11<H52),"OK","Incorrect date")
```

The data checking table is in cells G20 to H60, and the upper and lower limits used in the following formula are stored in cells G52 and H52, respectively. If you do not want the word OK to appear when the entry is correct, use " " instead of "OK".

## Use the NETWORKDAYS function to check work days and holidays

 When you enter dates used in scheduling, you may need to check that the date is a work day and not a weekend or holiday. There are two ways to do this.

The first method uses a formula that you enter. The following formula should be entered in a cell adjacent to the cell containing the date you want to check:

```
=IF(AND(WEEKDAY(C8)<>7,WEEKDAY(C8)<>1,
   ISERROR(MATCH(C8,Holidays,0))),"OK","Non-Workday")
```

In this example, cell C8 contains the date being checked. A list of holidays has been entered into a column on the worksheet and given the range name Holidays using Formula Define Name. You enter the dates in the list as you would normally, using a date format Excel recognizes.

Three conditions are checked to see whether the date is a work day. WEEKDAY(C8)<>7 checks that the date is not a Saturday. WEEKDAY(C8)<>1 checks that the date is not Sunday. The ISERROR and MATCH combination is true only when the date is not found in the Holidays range. The AND function ensures that all three conditions must be true for the date to be a work day.

The MATCH function checks whether C8 is in the Holidays list. If it is not in the list, MATCH results in an error. But the ISERROR function turns the error of not finding a matching holiday into TRUE. So the ISERROR and MATCH combination results in TRUE when the date is not found in the list of holidays.

Excel 4 has another, easier way to check work days. The Analysis ToolPak add-in includes the NETWORKDAYS function. This function checks the number of work days between dates, but you can use it also to check whether a date is a holiday.

To enter the NETWORKDAYS function, select the cell that you want to contain the check and choose the Formula Paste Function command. Select NETWORKDAYS from the Paste Function list, select the Paste Arguments check box, and choose OK. The function pastes into the cell as

```
=NETWORKDAYS(start_date,end_date,holidays)
```

Edit this function to become a formula, such as

```
=IF(NETWORKDAYS(C8,C8,Holidays)=1,"OK","Non-Workday")
```

C8, the date being checked, is used as both the start and end date. Holidays is the named range containing the list of holidays. If C8 contains a valid work day, NETWORKDAYS returns 1 because it is a single work day and OK is displayed.

## Use INDEX and MATCH to check data entries against a list

When you enter part numbers, descriptions, or other items, you may want to make sure that they are entered and spelled correctly. This is especially important later if you use the Formula Find command or must find, extract, or analyze data in a database.

You can use the INDEX and MATCH functions to check entered data against values in a list. Tests using LOOKUP, VLOOKUP, or HLOOKUP return a next closest match, but the MATCH and INDEX combinations indicate when no exact match is found. Another advantage is that the list containing valid entries can be in any order, whereas items in the LOOKUP, VLOOKUP, or HLOOKUP list must be in ascending order.

In the following example, the data being checked is in cell B22. This formula can be entered in any other cell:

```
=IF(ISERROR(MATCH(B22,List,0)),"Not in list","OK")
```

When B22 contains an entry that is not found in the named range List, the text Not in list is displayed. If the contents of B22 are found in the list, OK is displayed.

MATCH uses the form

```
MATCH(lookup_value,lookup_array,match_type)
```

The *lookup_value* is the value being checked against the list. The *lookup_array* is a reference to a range of cells or a named range (such as List in the example). The *match_type* in the example is 0, which means MATCH should look for only exact matches.

If MATCH cannot find an exact match, an error results. You are looking for cases where MATCH cannot find the entry in the list, so ISERROR changes the error from MATCH to TRUE. This causes `Not in list` to appear. If MATCH finds the entry in the list, `OK` appears. Use `""` instead of `"OK"` if you want no display for a valid entry.

## Use the accountant's keypad to enter decimal points automatically

An adding machine makes typing long lists of numbers faster because it can enter the decimal point automatically. When you type a number, the machine places the decimal two digits from the right. If you are accustomed to this feature, you can make Excel work the same way. To turn on the accountant's keypad so that decimals are automatically entered:

1. Choose **O**ptions **W**orkspace and select the Fixed Decimal check box.

2. In the **P**laces edit box, type the number of decimal places you want Excel to enter automatically. Choose OK.

Now when you need to type 98.67, for example, you can type **9867** and Excel enters the decimal when you press Enter.

## Protect formulas from overtyping

Two surveys in the corporate environment revealed that approximately 30% of worksheets contain some type of serious error. The most frequent cause of errors was accidentally typing a number over a formula, which permanently replaces the formula with the number. Any formula that references the result of the formula uses the number that replaced it.

Here are three ways to help keep your worksheets valid:

- Separate the data entry area from the formulas. If someone accidentally types a number in the wrong cell, the number won't be over a formula.

- Unprotect cells you want to enter data in and then protect the entire worksheet. This action prevents the operator from typing in any protected cell.

- Use a data entry macro to prompt the user for data. Data is typed in an INPUT or a custom dialog box, and the macro puts the data into the correct cell.

## Protect worksheets from data entry errors

If data is scattered throughout a worksheet or might be entered in the wrong location, format the worksheet so that data can be entered only in data entry cells. Protecting a worksheet is a two-step process. First you select cells that will be typed in and format them as unlocked. Then you turn on worksheet protection. While the worksheet protection is on, Excel enables you to type only in unlocked cells. To unlock cells in which you want to enter data:

1. Select the cells in which you want to enter data. Use Ctrl+click to select multiple cells at one time.

2. Choose the Format Cell Protection command.

3. Clear the Locked check box. (The default setting for cells is Locked.) Choose OK.

This action formats the cells so that they are unprotected when worksheet protection is turned on. At this point, you can still type in any worksheet cell. To turn on worksheet protection:

1. Choose the Options Protect Document command.

2. If you want to use a password so that unauthorized users cannot unlock the worksheet, type a password in the Password edit box.

3. Make sure that the Cells check box is selected. If you want to protect objects from moving, select the Objects check box. If you want to keep the window from being moved on-screen, select the Windows check box. Choose OK.

Tab or Shift+Tab now move between unlocked cells only. Use the arrow keys or mouse to select other cells. If you attempt to type in locked cells, an alert box warns you that you cannot.

To remove the protection from the worksheet so that you can type in any cell, choose Options Unprotect Document. If a password was used, you are prompted to type the password and choose OK.

## Restrict data entry to specific cells

 Excel 4 contains a macro function that makes data entry easier and safer. The ENTER.DATA function limits the movement in the window to an area you select and limits movement between cells to cells you format as unlocked.

ENTER.DATA works on the currently selected range of cells. Before the ENTER.DATA function runs, you or a macro must select a range of cells. The macros in figure 4.7 select the named ranges FormTop and FormBottom in the EMPLOYEE.XLS worksheet.

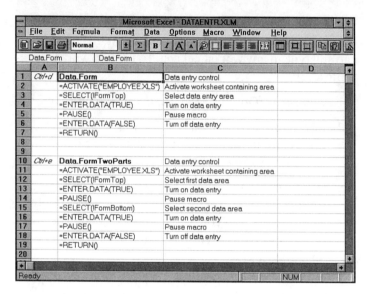

**Fig. 4.7** *Use the ENTER.DATA and PAUSE macro functions to create data entry forms.*

While ENTER.DATA is running, it limits scrolling through the window to the cells you formatted as unlocked with the Format Cell Protection command. Worksheet protection set with the Options Protect Document command does not have to be on. You can use the arrow keys, Tab, Shift+Tab, or the mouse to move between unlocked cells.

To turn off the data entry mode, press the Esc key. This returns the worksheet to normal operation.

The macros in figure 4.7 incorporate a second way to turn off the data entry mode, by pausing the macro with the PAUSE function. A floating Resume tool appears while the macro is paused. Click the Resume tool when you want to continue the macro. The ENTER.DATA(FALSE) function turns off the data entry mode just as if you pressed Esc.

The two macros in figure 4.7 operate on the worksheet EMPLOYEE.XLS. There are two ranges of data entry areas.

To create the data entry areas on your worksheet, use Formula Define Name to select and name one data entry range as FormTop. Use the same method to select and name a second data entry range as FormBottom. Within each range, use Format Cell Protection with the Locked check box cleared to format the cells in which you want to enter data. You do not have to turn on worksheet protection with Options Protect Document.

The first macro, Data.Form, is useful for a single data entry area. It begins by activating the EMPLOYEE.XLS worksheet. The SELECT function selects the FormTop range on the active worksheet. ENTER.DATA is then turned on by the TRUE argument. The PAUSE function puts the macro on hold while you enter data, and displays a floating Resume tool. Click the Resume tool or press Esc to continue the macro. The ENTER.DATA(FALSE) function turns off the data entry mode.

The second macro, Data.FormTwoParts, is useful for a data entry area with two separate areas. The first portion of the macro runs the same as the Data.Form macro, but following the first PAUSE, the macro selects a second data entry area and returns to the data entry mode. By repeating this process of selecting a range, going into data entry mode, and then pausing, you can set up a data entry macro for a multipart form.

Don't forget that the macros will not work unless you name the top cell in each of these macros, B1 and B10, with the Formula Define Name command. Make sure that you type the name of the macro in the Name edit box (if it is not already entered), select the Command option. If you want to use a shortcut key, enter a shortcut key in the Key edit box before you choose OK.

# 5

# Formatting Text, Dates, and Numbers

Your numbers may be accurate and your analysis valid,
your forecasts brilliant and your insight genius, but if the
results look drab or disheveled, you lose credibility and the
chance to get your ideas across. Excel enables you to give
your work the polished look that can make you stand out.
You can format text, numbers, and dates the way your
readers want and expect to see them. Excel has more
formatting and layout capability than other electronic
spreadsheets, and a few tips and tricks can help you get
the job accomplished quickly and more easily.

## Use the formatting toolbar to save time

In addition to the tools on the standard toolbar, Excel 4
contains many more tools to help you format numbers
and text. For example, the predefined Formatting toolbar
contains many formatting tools. You can add to the Formatting toolbar or create a custom toolbar with custom
formatting tools.

To display formatting tools and add them to any displayed toolbar:

1. Choose the Options Toolbars command.

2. Select the Customize button from the Toolbar dialog box.

3. From the Categories list, you can select either Formatting or Text Formatting to see additional formatting tools.

The tools in the Formatting category are used to add border outlines, a border to any edge, double-underline, and light or dark shadows. They also can apply the most recently used AutoStyle, format numbers for currency or percentage, and add or remove decimal places. You can also add a Style list.

The tools in the Text Formatting category enable you to boldface, italicize, underline, strike-through, or color characters. You can align text left, right, centered, or justified. Titles can be centered in the selection. You can change the font size, font name, or cell style by adding a pull-down list. Text size can be increased or decreased with the size tools. The last row of tools enables you to rotate text.

## Format multiple worksheets at one time

If you must format multiple worksheets, you can save time by formatting them as a group with the group edit feature. To use group edit:

1. Open or unhide all the worksheets you want to format.

2. Activate the worksheet in which you want to work and choose the Options Group Edit command.

3. In the Group Edit dialog box that appears, select the worksheets you want to format and choose OK. Each worksheet's name is appended with [Group] to indicate you are in group edit mode.

4. When you finish formatting, exit the group edit mode by activating any other worksheet.

## Center multiple titles over a varying number of columns

Many users are familiar with the Center across selection tool, but most do not realize it can center multiple titles across nonuniform selections. For example, in figure 5.1, when you center the titles in row 5, they appear as shown in row 10.

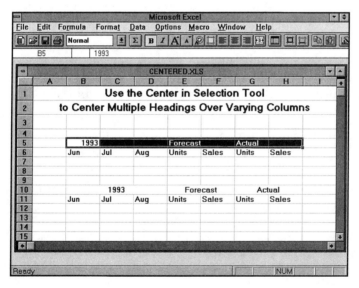

**Fig. 5.1** *Use the Center across selection tool to center headings across uneven columns.*

To center titles across the columns they head:

1. Type the title in the left cell of each row. Put it above the leftmost column of the columns it will be centered above. Leave blank cells until the next heading in that row.

2. Select all the cells across the headings.

3. Click the Center across selection tool. Alternatively, choose the Format Alignment command and select the Center across selection option.

Each heading is centered in the blank space preceding the next filled cell.

## Use cell styles to save formatting time

When formatting, you can save a tremendous amount of time by using cell styles. Cell styles are names that contain all the formatting characteristics for a cell. For example, the style named BottomLine could contain a numeric format for currency: two decimal places, 12-point Arial font, bold, with the top cell edge formatted with a double line.

There are two advantages to using styles. First, you can apply all the formatting characteristics in the style by just selecting a cell and choosing the style from the Style list in a toolbar. Second, when you use the Format Style command to change the formatting associated with a style, all cells with that style change also.

Rather than create a style with the Format Style command, you can more easily create a style by example. To do so:

1. Format a cell with the number format, borders, fonts, patterns, alignment, and protection you want.

2. Select the cell.

3. Type the name you want for that style in the Style list box in the standard, Formatting, or Microsoft Excel 3 toolbar, then press Enter. (The Style list box is to the left of the toolbar.)

To redefine a style, format a cell that already has that style. When you attempt to reapply the style to the cell you have reformatted, you are asked whether you want to redefine the existing style.

## Create a partial style that doesn't overwrite an existing format

Sometimes you want a cell style that retains certain existing format characteristics but changes others. For example, suppose that you want a style for currency that has a top double-line border for the cell containing a total, but you don't want this style to change the font or font size. This capability enables you to use the same style on parts of the worksheet that use different fonts.

To turn off the parts of a style that you don't want to apply:

1. Create the style using the style-by-example technique.

2. Choose the Format Style command.

3. Select the style's name in the Style Name box.

4. Choose the Define button. The Style dialog box expands as shown in figure 5.2.

5. Clear the check boxes in the Style Includes group for the formatting features that you do not want a style to override.

6. Choose OK.

**Fig. 5.2** *You can use styles to change selected formatting characteristics.*

## Merge styles from another worksheet

When you have spent a lot of time designing and refining styles for one worksheet, you will probably want the same styles on another worksheet. To merge styles from one worksheet into another:

1. Open both worksheets and activate the worksheet that will *receive* the styles.

2. Choose the Format Style command.

3. Choose the Define button, then the Merge button.

4. Select the worksheet that contains the styles you want merged, then choose OK to return to the Style dialog box. Choose Close to close the Style dialog box.

If the two worksheets contain styles with the same name, you are asked whether you want to merge the styles. If you do merge the styles, the incoming styles have precedence.

## Hide or display rows or columns quickly

When you work with a large report or database, sometimes it's convenient to hide the rows or columns you don't want to work in or don't want to print.

To hide rows:

1. Select a cell in each row to be hidden. Use Ctrl+click to select multiple nonadjacent cells.

2. Press Ctrl+9. (Use the 9 at the top of the keyboard.)

To unhide the rows, select the cells that span the rows you want to display, then press Shift+Ctrl+9. (Use the 9 at the top of the keyboard.)

To hide columns:

1. Select a cell in each column you want to hide. Use Ctrl+click to select multiple nonadjacent cells.

2. Press Ctrl+0. (Use the 0 at the top of the keyboard.)

To display hidden columns, select cells that span the hidden columns and press Shift+Ctrl+0. (Use the 0 at the top of the keyboard.)

## Use autoformats to save time

*Autoformats* are predefined formats that include currency, text, border, and color settings. Excel determines the location of the titles, data area, and summary rows, then applies the formats.

To apply an autoformat:

1. Select the range you want formatted. If the filled cells are touching, you can select just one of the cells.

2. Choose the Format AutoFormat command.

3. Select the format you want from the Table Format list, then choose OK.

You can see a sample of how the format will appear in the AutoFormat dialog box.

## Redefine the Normal style to change the default font

To change the default font in Excel, you redefine the Normal style. The easiest way to do this is to format a cell with the default format you want. Select that cell, then attempt to apply a Normal style to it using either the Style tool or the Format Style command. When Excel sees that the cell already has a Normal style but the formatting is different from the Normal definition, it asks whether you want to redefine the Normal definition. Choose the Yes button.

## Change the colors used by autoformat

You can change the colors used by autoformat by changing the color palette for the worksheet. Be careful, though, because the colors change wherever they are used on the worksheet. You can get around this by redefining colors not used by autoformat or patterns you have used on the worksheet. Colors you redefine appear as a number in formatting lists, such as the Font dialog box. This number is the location of the custom color in the color palette.

To change a color:

1. Display the worksheet.

2. Choose the Options Color Palette command.

3. Click the color you want to change in the Color Palette window, then select the Edit button.

4. Click the area of the Color Picker you want, then choose OK.

When you return to the Color Palette dialog box, write down the number of the color you redefined. The left column of colors are numbered from top to bottom as 1 to 8, and the right column of colors are numbered 9 to 16.

This helps you when you select a color from a format dialog box because custom colors appear with nondescriptive names, such as Color 11. Note that when you change the color palette, the colors used in 3-D Surface charts change also.

## Save time with numeric format shortcut keys

Some of the most common numeric formats have built-in shortcut keys, as shown in the following list:

| Format | Shortcut key |
|---|---|
| General | Shift+Ctrl+~ |
| #,##0.00 | Shift+Ctrl+! |
| $#,##0.00_);($#,##0.00) | Shift+Ctrl+$ |
| 0% | Shift+Ctrl+% |
| 0.00E+00 | Shift+Ctrl+^ |

## Create custom numeric and date formats

 If you don't like the numeric or date formats shown in the Number Format dialog box, you can create your own as follows:

1. Select the cell you want to format with a custom format.

2. Choose the Format Number command.

3. Figure 5.3 shows the Number Format dialog box that appears. Type the custom format in the Code edit box. Any custom formats you create on a worksheet are shown at the end of the Format Codes list, so you need to enter a custom format only once; thereafter, you can select it from the bottom of the list.

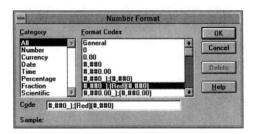

**Fig. 5.3**  *Enter almost any custom format in the Code edit box.*

Numeric formats can have four parts. Most of the pre-defined formats in the Number Format dialog box show only two parts. Each part of a custom numeric format applies to a different sign of number or text. The four parts of a custom numeric format are

*positive_format;negative_format;zero_format;text_format*

A semicolon separates the format for each part. The *text_format* part is used when text, and not a number or date, is typed in a cell. Date formats do not have multiple parts.

## Add text to a numeric format

You can add text to any numeric or date format by enclosing it in quotation marks. Type the text in the positive, negative, or zero value portions of the custom format.

For example:

```
#,##0;-#,##0;0
```

can be changed to

```
#,##0" Kph";#,##0" Kph";0" Kph"
```

## Use different colors for positive, negative, and zero values

You can add colors to numbers or text by including the color names in square brackets in the portions of the custom format. For example:

```
[Blue]#,##0" Kph";[Red]-#,##0" Kph";[Green]0" Kph"
```

The colors you can enclose in brackets are Black, White, Red, Green, Blue, Yellow, Magenta, and Cyan.

You also can use [Color#], where # is the number of a color from the color palette. Display and edit the custom color palette by choosing the Options Color Palette command. The colors are numbered from 1 to 8 on the left and 9 to 16 on the right.

## Use Precision as Displayed to avoid totals that appear to be incorrect

When you format numbers, you change their displayed and printed appearance, but you do not change the underlying value used in calculations. For this reason, a column of formatted numbers may appear to be calculated incorrectly—the displayed details are rounded according to the formatting, but the calculations are performed on the unrounded numbers stored in the cell.

To prevent this problem and the embarrassment it can cause during presentations:

1. Choose the Options Calculation command.

2. Select the Precision as Displayed check box.

3. Choose OK. An alert box warns that Data will permanently lose accuracy. This means that constant numbers you entered will be rounded to match their formatting.

In nearly all financial worksheets, you will want to operate with the Precision as Displayed feature turned on.

## Create a custom format to align a column of numbers

Some numeric formats cause the positive and negative numbers to fall out of alignment in a column. For example,

```
#,##0;<#,##0>;0
```

misaligns the positive and negative numbers when a column is left aligned. This is because the negative number has a trailing character, in this case the right angle bracket (>).

To compensate for characters that may be missing between portions of a format, use the underscore character (_) to indicate the width of the invisible placeholder. Type the character you want to use as an invisible placeholder after the underscore character. For example, to correct the preceding format, use this format:

```
#,##0_>;<#,##0>;0
```

## Create a custom date format to show abbreviations or full spellings

The format of a custom date changes depending on the number of letters used to indicate the day, month, or year portion. Type your custom date format in the Code edit box of the Format Number dialog box. For example:

| Format | Produces |
|--------|----------|
| m/d/yy | 8/6/93 |
| mm/dd/yyyy | 08/06/1993 |
| mmm d, yyyy | Aug 6, 1993 |
| mmmm d, yyyy | August 6, 1993 |
| dddd, mmm d, yy | Friday, Aug 6, 93 |
| "Today is"mmmm d, yyyy | Today is August 6, 1993 |

## Use a custom format to round numbers to display or print thousands or millions

You can round a number up by a thousand or a million for display and printing but still have the actual number in the cell for calculations if you use the correct custom format. For example:

| Number in cell | Format | Displays or prints | Magnitude |
|----------------|--------|--------------------|-----------|
| 999,888,777 | ###, | 999889 | Thousands |
| 999,888,777 | ###,, | 1000 | Millions |

# 6

## CHAPTER

# Working with Formulas

Formulas are the heart and soul of your worksheet. If you build many worksheets or macros in Excel, you will appreciate any tricks that help you build worksheets faster and with fewer errors. This chapter describes tips to help you enter, edit, and duplicate formulas. Some formulas in this chapter may help you solve common business problems.

## Use F4 to change between relative and absolute cell references

You don't have to type the dollar signs to change a cell reference from a relative reference to an absolute or a mixed reference. When the insertion point is next to a cell reference, whether you are entering or editing, you can press the F4 key to enter cell references. Each press of the key cycles it to another combination of dollar signs. For example, pressing F4 cycles the relative reference B12 through $B$12, B$12, $B12, and back to B12.

## Use Ctrl+' (apostrophe) or the Clipboard to copy a formula without references adjusting

Sometimes you must experiment with a formula by changing it, but you want to be safe and leave the original formula untouched. You can't copy and paste the formula to another cell and experiment with it there, because that process adjusts the relative cell references.

You can copy a formula in a new cell—without the formula adjusting—in two ways. If a blank cell is under the cell that contains the formula, select the blank cell and press Ctrl+' (apostrophe). This action copies the formula without adjusting the cell references.

**Caution:** Do not use the Ctrl+' (apostrophe) shortcut key when entering data. In most data entry situations, you want the relative references of a formula to adjust, which this shortcut does not do.

The following steps describe the other way to copy a formula without the references adjusting:

1. Select the cell containing the formula.

2. Click in front of the equal sign in the formula bar and drag to the end of the formula so that the entire formula is selected.

3. Choose the Edit Copy command to copy the formula to the Clipboard.

4. Select the cell where you want the formula to be copied and choose the Edit Paste command. This command pastes the formula without adjusting relative cell references.

## Use the Clipboard to copy and paste in the formula bar

You can cut, copy, and paste in a formula bar just as you would in a miniature word processor. This capability is helpful when you are building complex formulas that share a common part or reorganizing a formula.

To cut or copy using the Clipboard, select the portion in the formula bar you want to cut or copy, then choose the Edit Cut command (Ctrl+X) or the Edit Copy command (Ctrl+C).

If you want to paste in the same formula, just move the insertion point to where you want to paste and choose the Edit Paste command (Ctrl+V). If you want to paste into another formula, select the cell containing that formula, move the insertion point in its formula bar to where you want to paste, and choose the Edit Paste command.

## Use the Clipboard to copy and paste in Excel dialog boxes

Sometimes you can save time by copying and pasting in dialog boxes. The Edit commands don't work in dialog boxes. The editing shortcut keys, however, do work in many dialog boxes. For example, if you need to find all occurrences of a complex range name or a portion of a formula:

1. Copy a portion of a formula or text into the Clipboard as described in the preceding tip.

2. Display the dialog box into which you want to paste the formula or text.

3. Select the edit box into which you want to paste and press Ctrl+V.

If you want to copy from within a dialog box, select the characters and press Ctrl+C. To cut from within a dialog box, select the characters and press Ctrl+X.

## Paste function arguments rather than memorize them

When using Excel's multitude of worksheet functions, it's hard to remember the order in which arguments are placed in parentheses. Thank heaven you don't have to. Instead, when you need a function:

1. Paste the function and its arguments by choosing the Formula Paste Function command (Shift+F3).

2. Select the function you want from the Paste Function list.

3. Make sure that the Paste Arguments check box is turned on, then choose OK.

Excel pastes the function and inserts a text description of each argument within the parentheses.

## Double-click to select an argument or part of a formula

Do you remember using the Del or Backspace key to slowly delete an argument or part of a formula and then typing the correction? Instead, you can double-click any word, cell reference, range name, or argument. The entire element is selected. Double-click and drag to select multiple elements.

Double-clicking selects touching characters bordered by spaces, commas, or math operators. When the entire item is selected, you can replace it by typing, clicking a cell, or pasting a range name or function. (Press F3 to paste names or Shift+F3 to paste functions.)

To select multiple elements without a mouse, move the insertion point to the beginning of a portion of text, a cell reference, a range name, or an argument. Select across it by pressing Ctrl+Shift+right arrow. Press Ctrl+Shift+right arrow multiple times to select multiple words.

## Use Formula Replace to change multiple formulas

When you are using similar formulas in worksheets or macros, you can speed up your work by using the Formula Replace command instead of retyping each formula. For example, suppose a macro has many SET.VALUE functions that set the defaults for a dialog box. The FORMULA functions that transfer data from the same dialog box use almost the same form and may act on the same references or range names. Instead of entering all the SET.VALUE functions and then typing all the FORMULA functions:

1. Copy the SET.VALUE functions to where you want the FORMULA functions.

2. Select all the SET.VALUE functions.

3. Use the Formula Replace command to replace SET.VALUE with FORMULA.

4. Make sure that the Look at Part option is selected, then choose OK.

## Use Formula Replace to recalculate a portion of a worksheet

You can recalculate a portion of a worksheet rather than the entire worksheet. To do so:

1. Choose the Options Calculation command, and make sure that the worksheet is in manual calculation mode.

2. Select the area you want to affect, and choose the Formula Replace command.

3. In the Find What edit box, type an equal sign (=).

4. Type an equal sign (=) in the Replace With edit box.

5. Make sure that the Look at Part option is selected, then choose Replace All.

The selected area recalculates because the Replace command is re-entering each formula when it replaces the equal sign.

## Paste names from other worksheets into formulas

When you build macros or formulas that involve data from other worksheets, you must use the range names that are on the other worksheets. Trying to memorize these names and typing them into formulas can give you a worksheet fraught with errors. A much better method is to paste the names used in the other worksheets.

To paste a name from one worksheet into another:

1. Select the cell and type an equal sign. Alternatively, if you are in a formula, move the insertion point to where you want the name.

2. Activate the worksheet or macro sheet containing the name by pressing Ctrl+F6 to switch to the next sheet or choosing a specific sheet from the Window menu. (The Window menu works even though you are in the middle of editing.)

3. Press the F3 key or choose the Formula Paste Name command.

4. The Paste Name dialog box appears. Select the name you want to paste and choose OK.

5. Continue to build the formula or switch between worksheets.

6. When you press Enter, the worksheet or macro sheet containing the formula reactivates and shows the finished formula.

**Note:** The Paste Name dialog box will not display if no names are defined on the active worksheet.

## Use the Name Changer to change names

Unless you are near-perfect, you will probably change your mind about your abbreviations for some names in large worksheets. To change the names manually, you must redefine the new names, change all the formulas that used the old name, then delete the old name—and hope you corrected all instances of the old name.

To change names with the Name Changer add-in:

1. Choose the Formula Change Name command.

2. The Rename a Name dialog box appears. In the From list, select the name you want changed. In the To list, type the new name.

3. Choose Rename.

The Name Changer redefines the name, replaces the old name in all the formulas, then deletes the old name. However, if you created the names from text labels in cells using the Formula Create Names command, the text labels are not updated to reflect the new names.

**Note:** If the Formula Change Name command is not available, use the Options Add-ins command to add CHANGER.XLA to Excel. The CHANGER.XLA add-in is found in the EXCEL\LIBRARY directory. If your computer

does not have the LIBRARY directory or the
CHANGER.XLA file, get your original Excel installation
disks and rerun the installation using the Custom installation option. You do not need to reinstall all of Excel; install
only the LIBRARY.

## Calculate part of a formula to check for errors

 When a formula is not working correctly, you
may want to calculate sections of the formula to
check for mistakes. When troubleshooting, it is
usually best to start by calculating smaller inside portions
of a formula, then work outward to the entire formula.

To calculate part of a formula:

1. Select the cell containing the formula.

2. Click the formula bar or press F2.

3. Select the section of the formula you want to
   calculate.

4. Press the F9 key to see the result of the selection.

5. When you finish examining the partial results, press
   the Esc key so that the altered formula does not replace the original formula.

This tip doesn't work if the selected piece refers to an un-
opened worksheet or if a selected macro function requires
the worksheet to be active when the selected function
calculates.

## Select cells leading to or from a formula to find errors

When troubleshooting formulas, it's often helpful to know
which formulas or data feed into the selected formula

(precedents) and which formulas depend on the selected formula (dependents). In this way, you can track where an error came from or went to.

One way to see precedence or dependence cells is to select the formula in question and choose the Formula Select Special command. Then select the Precedents or Dependents options. For each option, you can choose to see the cells that directly precede or depend (the Direct Only option) or all cells that precede or depend (the All Levels option).

A faster way to see what feeds into or out of a formula is to select the formula, then press one of these shortcut keys:

| | |
|---|---|
| Ctrl+[ | To see cells that feed directly into the formula |
| Ctrl+Shift+{ | To see all cells that eventually feed into the formula |
| Ctrl+] | To see cells that depend directly on the formula |
| Ctrl+Shift+} | To see all cells that eventually depend on the formula |

## View or print the formulas in a worksheet

You can display or print worksheet formulas instead of results. To do so:

1. Choose the **O**ptions **D**isplay command.

2. Select the Formulas check box.

3. Choose OK.

The columns automatically double in width to show more of the formulas. If you change a column width, it is changed in the normal display also.

To quickly switch between displaying formulas and results, press Ctrl+' (back apostrophe). The back apostrophe is located on the same key as the tilde (~).

## Use group edit to enter formulas in multiple worksheets simultaneously

If you must enter the same formula in more than one worksheet (in the same location), you can do so all at once by using group edit mode.

To enter the same formula into the same location in multiple worksheets:

1. Open all the worksheets that will receive the same formula. Activate the worksheet that's the easiest to use for entering the formula.

2. Choose the Options Group Edit command.

3. The Group Edit dialog box appears. From the Select Group list, select the worksheets that you want in the group. Ctrl+click to select multiple worksheets.

4. Choose OK.

All worksheets in the group display [Group] in their title bars. Exit group edit mode by activating any other worksheet.

## Find the chain of connected formulas in a circular reference

A *circular reference* is when two or more formulas refer back to themselves. (Imagine it as a snake eating its tail.) Formulas A, B, and C are involved in a circular reference, for example, when A uses B's results, B uses C's results, and C uses A's results. Because all the results depend on each other, strange things can happen when the worksheet recalculates. You should investigate circular reference errors to determine whether they are benign or malignant. (Sometimes circular references are useful in solving iterative problems.)

When a formula is entered that closes the chain and initially creates a circular reference, an alert box appears with the message Cannot resolve circular reference. When you choose OK, the Status bar at the bottom of the screen shows a message such as Circular: A12. A12 is the cell of the last entry that created the circular reference.

Do not just delete the cell shown in the Circular message. There may be many cells that reference each other. To find all the cells in a circular error:

1. Select the cell shown in the Status bar.

2. Choose the Formula Select Special command.

3. Select either the Precedents or Dependents option, then select the All Levels option.

4. Choose OK, and all the cells that reference each other will be selected.

5. To examine each formula while keeping them all selected, press the Tab key to move between them. Look for a cell reference that somehow refers back to itself.

If after choosing the Formula Select Special command only the original cell is selected, its formula is referring to the cell in which it resides—it is trying to calculate a new result based on its own result.

With a complicated circular reference, use the Audit add-in for a printed report of all cells involved in the circular reference, their formulas, and their results. To do so:

1. Choose the Formula Worksheet Auditor command.

2. The Worksheet Auditor dialog box appears. Select the Generate Audit Report option, and choose OK.

3. The Audit Report dialog box appears. Select only the Circular References check box, then choose OK.

In large worksheets with complicated circular errors, generating the circular reference error report may take as long as half an hour.

**Note:** If the Formula Worksheet Auditor command is not available, use the Options Add-ins command to add the AUDIT.XLA add-in to Excel. The AUDIT.XLA add-in is in the EXCEL\LIBRARY directory. If your computer does not have the LIBRARY directory or the AUDIT.XLA file, get your original Excel installation disks and rerun the installation using the Custom installation option. You do not need to reinstall all of Excel; install only the LIBRARY.

## Search for exclamation marks to find formulas linked to other worksheets

The exclamation mark is always used as a separator between file names and cell reference in external references. Thus, you can find any formula linked to another worksheet by searching for the exclamation mark. To search:

1. Use the Formula Find command.

2. Type ! in the Find What dialog box.

3. Make sure that the Look in Formulas and Look at Part options are selected.

4. Choose OK to find the next linked formula.

5. To continue with the same search, press F7.

## Use the AutoSum tool to total multiple columns or rows

The AutoSum tool is a useful way of quickly summing a column or row. But there are tricks that make using AutoSum even faster. You can enter the SUM function into multiple cells at one time. If you are totaling columns, all the columns must have the same number of cells, but the columns of numbers do not have to be aligned. The selected cells at the bottom of the columns will receive totals when you double-click the AutoSum tool.

If you are totaling rows, all the rows must have the same number of cells, but the rows do not have to be aligned. To enter multiple totals at one time, select all the cells where you want the total, then double-click the AutoSum tool.

## Don't let cell widths hamper your formulas

Some reports require very specific formatting. This is a problem when a large result does not fit in a narrow cell. When a number or date is too wide to fit in a cell, the cell displays ###.

Resolve this problem by putting the formula in a TEXT function. Figure 6.1 shows how formula results can fit in narrow cells and be aligned as you would align text, as follows:

| | |
|---|---|
| Column B | This is where you enter the numbers. |
| Column D | Contains the TEXT function that converts the numbers in the B column to text-numbers. |
| Column F | Shows the formula in column D. |

Note that the B column cell references in the TEXT functions can be complete formulas rather than a reference to a cell that contains a formula.

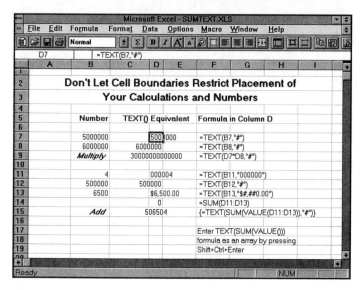

**Fig. 6.1** *Use the TEXT function to put numeric formulas in narrow cells.*

## Calculate a range of data using a single array formula

You can do a lot of math in a single cell if you understand how to use array formulas. For example, in figure 6.2, the more usual method of calculating total dollars sold is shown in cell E10. But this method requires first multiplying the quantity and price to produce subtotals in cells E6:E9. That takes up room on the worksheet.

You can use an array formula to perform—in a single cell—many calculations on multiple ranges. The formula in cell E12 performs the same multiplication and total as the formula in E10, but all the calculations are performed in one cell. The formula in E12 is shown in G12. The formula in E12 was entered as an array formula by typing

```
=SUM(C6:C9*D6:D9)
```

and pressing Ctrl+Shift+Enter, which surrounds the formula with braces, {}.

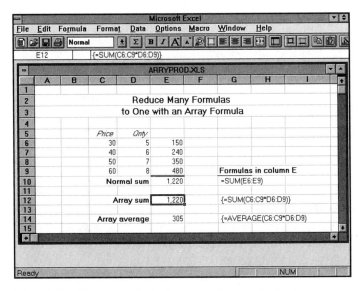

**Fig. 6.2** *Use array formulas to perform calculations on ranges in a single cell.*

**Note:** You cannot create an array formula by typing the braces. The braces are entered automatically when you press Ctrl+Shift+Enter.

The array formula works by first multiplying each cell in the C6:C9 range times the corresponding cell in the D6:D9 range. This action produces an array of multiplication results. You can see these results if, after entering the formula with Ctrl+Shift+Enter, you select the terms C6:C9*D6:D9 in the formula bar and press the Calculate key (F9). The results appear in the formula bar as

`=SUM({150;240;350;480})`

Press Esc to preserve the original formula. Finally, the SUM function in cell E12 totals the array of multiplication results.

Cell E14 in figure 6.2 shows an average of products created with an array formula. Again, the braces are entered automatically when you press Ctrl+Shift+Enter. This formula first does a cell-by-cell multiplication of the two ranges. The AVERAGE function then averages the results of the multiplication.

## Calculate the last day of the month

Excel 4 can calculate the end of a month by tricking the DATE function into backing up one day from the first of the following month. This procedure also works to calculate February 29 in leap years. To calculate the end of a month, use the following formula:

DATE(year,month+1,0)

For example, the formula

DATE(93,4+1,0)

results in 4/30/93. You also can use cell references or formulas instead of numbers. For example:

DATE(B12,B13+1,0)

## Calculate the last work day of the month

For invoice due dates, payrolls, or tax calculations, you may need to figure out the last work day of each month. The WORKDAY function can do it for you, by finding a work day that is a specified number of work days in the future or past.

You can calculate the last work day of the month by giving WORKDAY the last day of the month as the *start_date* and then asking for the closest prior work day. To do this, use the following formula

```
=WORKDAY(start_date+1,-1,holidays)
```

This formula adds 1 to the *start_date*. The –1 as the day argument asks WORKDAY to find the next prior work day. If you use the last day of the month as the *start_date* argument, this formula calculates the last work day of the month. Combine the preceding formula with the tip that calculates the last day of a month to produce a formula that calculates the last work day of the month:

```
=WORKDAY(DATE(year,month+1,0)+1,-1,holidays)
```

The *year* and *month* arguments are integer numbers. The *holidays* argument is a range that contains the dates excluded from work days.

# 7

# Outlining, Consolidating, and Tabulating Data

When you have a lot of data, whether in a database or worksheet format, consider using the outlining and crosstab features of Excel for compiling, analyzing, and reporting the results. Other useful Excel features are the Scenario Manager, which can help you manage multiple sets of input data, and the Consolidation command, which you can use to accumulate data from multiple worksheets.

## Use Scenario Manager to check input results

If you must generate different scenarios for your worksheet, such as best case, worst case, and most probable case, investigate the Scenario Manager. The Scenario Manager is available by choosing the Formula Scenario command. The Scenario Manager is an add-in, so if you do not have the Formula Scenario command available, choose the Options Add-ins command to add the SCENARIO.XLA file.

The Scenario Manager stores named sets of input data and the output results. To rerun a scenario, you just open the Scenario Manager and select the scenario by name. You can see the changes in the worksheet on-screen or print only the input data and the results.

## Name worksheet cells for a readable scenario summary

If you choose the Summary button in the Scenario Manager, Excel generates a summary report like the one in figure 7.1. The report shows the input data and the results for the scenario chosen from the Scenario Manager.

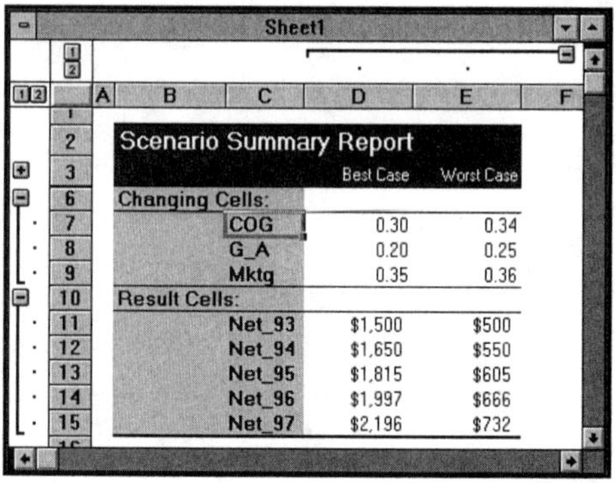

**Fig. 7.1** *Name input and result cells for easy-to-read reports from the Scenario Manager.*

If you do not use named ranges on your worksheet, the summary report from the Scenario Manager is almost inscrutable, showing input cells and result cells with their cell references, such as $B$12 or $AC$15:$AF$15. To use such a report, you need the original worksheet—or an incredible memory.

To produce a readable summary like the one in figure 7.1, you name your input cells and result cells before generating the summary report. You can name cells manually with the Formula Define Name command. Alternatively, you can use the Formula Create Names command to create multiple names using the text labels in the worksheet. The summary report includes the range names, even if you create the names after the scenarios are built and stored in the Scenario Manager.

## Build an outline toolbar for easier outlines

The Excel 4 standard toolbar does not have the collection of tools you need to work with outlines. Display the Microsoft Excel 3 toolbar, or create a custom toolbar that contains the outline tools from the Utility category of the Customize toolbar dialog box.

## Use the Excel 3 Select as Displayed tool to print restricted outlines

Interpreting an outlined area of the worksheet can be confusing if you print or chart a selection when only a few outline levels are displayed. Suppose that an outline has five levels of row headings, but only the top two levels are displayed. If you select this data and print it or chart it, Excel uses data from the full five levels of row headings.

To print or chart only the outline level you want, you must use the Select as Displayed tool. (The Select as Displayed tool is on the Excel 3 toolbar to the left of the AutoSum tool, and looks like four dark cells with spaces between them. If you want to add it to an Excel 4 toolbar, display the Customize toolbar dialog box and drag the Select as Displayed tool from the Utility category to a toolbar.) Then, follow these steps:

1. Display the outline with the level you want.

2. Select the data you are interested in.

3. Click the Select as Displayed tool. Notice that the selection changes as though the interior of each cell, but not the spaces between cells, is selected.

4. Continue with your normal charting or printing procedure.

## Use Crosstab ReportWizard to create database reports

 The Crosstab ReportWizard is one of the most exciting features added to Excel 4. If you work with databases or information downloaded from a mainframe, investigate the types of reports the Crosstab ReportWizard can build for you. Reports from the Crosstab ReportWizard can be linked to the original data so that changes in the data are reflected in the cross-tabulation. You also can display the detail that went into a cross-tabulation by double-clicking a summary result. Figure 7.2 shows a cross-tabulation report generated by the Crosstab ReportWizard from a database in Excel.

To use the Crosstab ReportWizard:

1. Select the database and database field names on your worksheet.

2. Choose the **Data Set Database** command. This command gives the database the name *Database.*

3. Choose the **Data Crosstab** command. When the Crosstab ReportWizard screen appears, follow the directions on the left side of the screen.

If Crosstab ReportWizard is not installed, rerun the Excel installation diskettes. Choose the Custom installation process and install only the Crosstab ReportWizard.

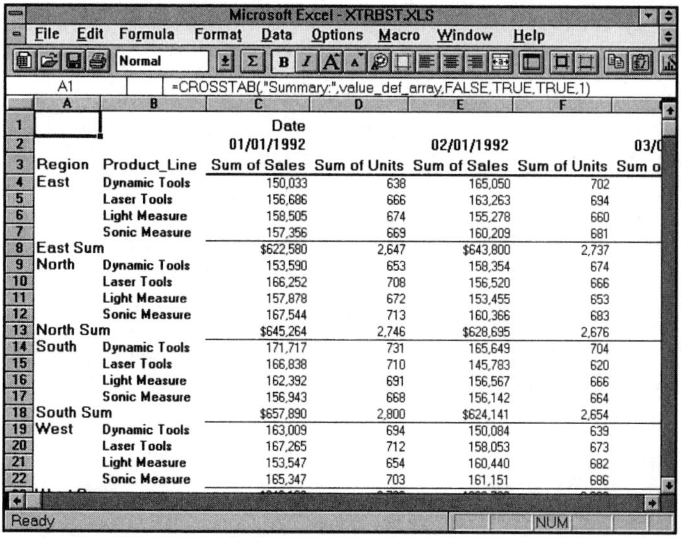


| | A | B | C | D | E | F | |
|---|---|---|---|---|---|---|---|
| 1 | | | Date | | | | |
| 2 | | | 01/01/1992 | | 02/01/1992 | | 03/0 |
| 3 | Region | Product_Line | Sum of Sales | Sum of Units | Sum of Sales | Sum of Units | Sum o |
| 4 | East | Dynamic Tools | 150,033 | 638 | 165,050 | 702 | |
| 5 | | Laser Tools | 156,686 | 666 | 163,263 | 694 | |
| 6 | | Light Measure | 158,505 | 674 | 155,278 | 660 | |
| 7 | | Sonic Measure | 157,356 | 669 | 160,209 | 681 | |
| 8 | East Sum | | $622,580 | 2,647 | $643,800 | 2,737 | |
| 9 | North | Dynamic Tools | 153,590 | 653 | 158,354 | 674 | |
| 10 | | Laser Tools | 166,252 | 708 | 156,520 | 666 | |
| 11 | | Light Measure | 157,878 | 672 | 153,455 | 653 | |
| 12 | | Sonic Measure | 167,544 | 713 | 160,366 | 683 | |
| 13 | North Sum | | $645,264 | 2,746 | $628,695 | 2,676 | |
| 14 | South | Dynamic Tools | 171,717 | 731 | 165,649 | 704 | |
| 15 | | Laser Tools | 166,838 | 710 | 145,783 | 620 | |
| 16 | | Light Measure | 162,392 | 691 | 156,567 | 666 | |
| 17 | | Sonic Measure | 156,943 | 668 | 156,142 | 664 | |
| 18 | South Sum | | $657,890 | 2,800 | $624,141 | 2,654 | |
| 19 | West | Dynamic Tools | 163,009 | 694 | 150,084 | 639 | |
| 20 | | Laser Tools | 167,265 | 712 | 158,053 | 673 | |
| 21 | | Light Measure | 153,547 | 654 | 160,440 | 682 | |
| 22 | | Sonic Measure | 165,347 | 703 | 161,151 | 686 | |

**Fig. 7.2** *Use the Crosstab ReportWizard to create many types of reports and analyses.*

## Limit the data analyzed by the Crosstab ReportWizard

The Crosstab ReportWizard works on the data that has the range name Database. If you operate the Crosstab ReportWizard without restriction, it analyzes all data in the database. For example, if your database has thousands of rows of data on four sales regions collected over the past three years, the Crosstab ReportWizard analyzes and reports on all the data. This analysis requires additional time, and may not produce the report you want.

To restrict the data that the Crosstab ReportWizard uses for analyzing and reporting, create a Criteria range on the database worksheet as you would create a Criteria range for a normal Excel database.

To specify the data you want the Crosstab ReportWizard to work on, enter your criteria in the Criteria range. Before starting the Crosstab ReportWizard to build your report, use the Data Find command to see if your criteria finds the type of data you want in your report.

## Group crosstab results into date groups

If your reports and analyses use data that covers a range of time, you will probably want the data analyzed according to groups of time, such as days, weeks, months, or quarters. For example, sales data may be entered every day, infrequent days, or weekly, but you need to see it totaled into groups of weeks, months, or quarters. The Crosstab ReportWizard does this for you.

After you select your Row or Column Categories that include dates, choose the Options button in the lower right corner of the ReportWizard. In the window that appears, pull down the In Groups Of list to select the time group and the time or date frequency by which you want your data grouped.

## Limit time spans in crosstab reports

If you did not use a Criteria range to limit the data on which the Crosstab ReportWizard works, you can specify a start and stop date for the data. After you select your row or column headings from the Row or Column Category Options window, choose the Options button. In the Category Options window, enter the start date in the Starting at edit box and enter the end date in the Ending at edit box.

## Modify an existing crosstab to save time

If you want to rebuild a crosstab report with different data fields, date groups, or restrictions, you can modify the report rather than create a new one. It is very easy to use the Crosstab ReportWizard to modify the report. Make sure that the original database worksheet is open, then activate the worksheet containing the crosstab report. Choose the Data Crosstab command. When the Crosstab ReportWizard appears, choose the Modify Current Crosstab button.

## Recalculate a crosstab report instead of rebuilding it

If data in the crosstab report has changed, you don't need to rebuild the report. Open the worksheet containing the database, then activate the worksheet containing the crosstab report and choose the Data Crosstab command. When the Crosstab ReportWizard appears, choose the Recalculate Current Crosstab button.

## Use formula names to retrieve or use crosstab results

If you want to be able to retrieve data from the crosstab report by typing English-like names, choose the Set Table Creation Options button in the final Crosstab Report-Wizard window. The Create Options window appears. Select Yes for the option with the heading `Define names for use in formulas?`.

When the Crosstab ReportWizard creates the cross-tabulation report, the rows, columns, and the entire range have understandable names—assuming that you under-stood the headings in your database. You can go to one of the named ranges by pressing F5 (the Goto key), selecting a name, and choosing OK. Note that the entire cross-tabulation report is always named Crosstab_range.

Rows are given a label derived from the headings used in each row. Columns likewise are given names derived from column headings. You can use these names in formulas to reference specific data or with the F5 key to go to a specific cell.

For example, if an entire row in the report is named Laser_Tools and an entire column is named Jun93, you can reference the data where the row and column cross by using the intersect operator, which is a space. If you want a cell to show two times the Laser_Tools sum for the month of June 1993, the formula is

```
=(Laser_Tools Jun93)*2
```

That's so easy to understand it almost makes worksheets easy to use. (Notice the space between the names Laser_Tools and Jun93.)

To go to the intersection of Aug93 and Grand_total, for example, you press the F5 key, type **Grand_total Aug93** in the **R**eference edit box, then choose OK.

### Double-click to see the detail of a crosstab result

EIS (Enterprise Information Systems) enables corporations to access and analyze the data in corporate computers more easily. Cross-tabulations and charts are a major part of the information displayed on EIS screens. Only a few years ago, the software and consulting to build this type of system would cost hundreds of thousands of dollars. Now the same results can be produced with Excel and a few months of macro development.

One EIS showstopper is the capability to show the detail that goes into a summary result by double-clicking the summary number. When you "drill-down" like this, the detail numbers appear in their own worksheet. When you use the Crosstab ReportWizard to create reports from Excel databases, the drill-down capability is built in.

If you want your cross-tabulation to have drill-down capability, follow these steps:

1. In the Final window of the Crosstab ReportWizard, choose the Set Table Creation Options button.

2. The Create Options window appears. Choose Yes for the option with the following heading: `Define Double-Click in the crosstab range to display source data`.

3. Choose OK.

4. Choose the Create It button to create your report.

If you want to see the detail information that makes up a summary item, double-click the item. Excel builds a report on another worksheet, showing the data that went into that summary item. For example, if you double-click a quarterly total for the Laser tools product line, Excel builds and displays a worksheet of the products in the Laser tools product line and the sales for the quarter. This detail report is a separate worksheet, so you can change data in it without changing the original data in the database.

# 8

## CHAPTER

# Writing Reports

Get the numbers right, get the report out on schedule, and make the report presentable. These tasks can be formidable. You expect the analysis to require thoughtful work, but sometimes the layout of a report slows you down. The tips in this chapter can help you get reports finished faster, make them look better, and highlight the veracity of your numbers.

For these tips, you must insert columns in the report and copy formulas, which results in extra work if you create the report directly from your database. Instead, create your report using an extract or copy of the database.

### Use a formula to hide or display rows and columns

You can calculate which rows of a report or database to hide with the following trick. This is useful for exception reports, when the order of records changes, or when the specifications for the report change. No matter how the data changes, it will be easy for you to rerun the report and hide just the rows you want.

It is just as easy to unhide the hidden rows, returning the report to its original condition. You can use this same trick to hide columns.

This technique uses a formula that you copy down the side of the database. The formula checks to see which rows do *not* meet the specifications of what you want to display.

Figure 8.1 shows the light machinery database. The selected cells are in the rows that will be hidden. The only rows that will display are the rows in which the sales are greater than the number in cell B8. This is accomplished by copying the formula in cell A12 down the side of the database.

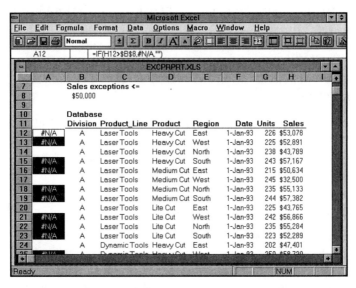

**Fig. 8.1** *Selectively hide rows or columns with the correct formula and two commands.*

The formula in cell A12 is

```
=IF(H12>$B$8,#N/A,"")
```

This formula matches the sales in the first database row against the amount typed in cell B8. You must make B8 an absolute reference so it will not change when the formula is copied down the side of the database. The formula results in the #N/A error when sales are greater than $50,000—these are the rows you want to hide.

Select all the rows to hide by selecting column A. Then choose the Formula Select Special command. In the Select Special dialog box that appears, choose the Formulas option and clear all the options except Errors. Then choose OK. This selects all the cells that contain #N/A, and these cells are in the rows you want to hide. Hide these rows by choosing the Format Row Height command and choosing the Hide button.

To return the report to its original condition so that all rows are displayed, you can repeat the process but choose the Unhide button in the Row Height dialog box, or you can select the entire database and choose the Unhide button.

When you perform this technique with macros, you gain expanding and contracting capabilities like the outline feature, but with more flexibility.

## Use a formula to check breaks and calculate subtotals

Many reports are easier to read if you show a subtotal when a category changes. One simple method that doesn't involve macros is shown in figure 8.2. To use this method, your database or list must first be sorted based on the column by which you are grouping subtotals.

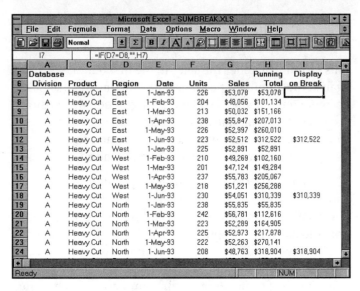

**Fig. 8.2** *Create subtotals and totals on breaks using an IF function.*

Column H contains running totals that start over when the region changes. To produce these running totals by region, enter the following formula in cell H7:

```
=G7
```

In cell H8, enter the formula

```
=IF(D8=D7,G8+H7,G8)
```

This checks whether the region for this row is the same as the region for the row above. If the region is the same, the running total above (in cell H7) is added to the current sales in cell G8. If the current row and the row above are in different regions, a new total appears in cell G8. The formula in cell H8 must be copied down the entire height of the report.

To display subtotals only when the region changes, you need another column. This column is shown in column I. The formula in I7 is

```
=IF(D7=D8," ",H7)
```

Notice that this formula checks the region for its row against the region for the row below. If the region for the row below is the same region, nothing is displayed. If the region below is different, the subtotal in the adjacent row is displayed. Copy this formula down the entire height of the report.

If you want only the subtotals in column I to display, hide column H.

## Use an IF formula to show titles and labels only when they change

Many reports look better if repetitive text does not appear. For example, the report in figure 8.2 might look better if the *A* for division appeared only at the beginning of the A division, the *Heavy Cut* appeared only at the beginning of the Heavy Cut group, and the *East, West, North,* and *South* labels appeared only at the start of their groups.

You must insert a column for each column in which you want labels displayed only when there is a change. In this column, you type a formula similar to the formula for I7 in the preceding tip. The database or list must be sorted by the column containing the items by which you are grouping.

For example, figure 8.3 shows a report in which the region displays in column E in the first row only when a new region begins. Enter the formula

```
=IF(D7<>D6,D7," ")
```

in cell E7 and copy it down the height of the database.

| | A | C | D | E | F | G | H | I |
|---|---|---|---|---|---|---|---|---|
| 5 | Database | | | | | | | |
| 6 | Division | Product | Region | Region | Date | Units | Sales | |
| 7 | A | Heavy Cut | East | East | 1-Jan-93 | 226 | $53,078 | |
| 8 | A | Heavy Cut | East | | 1-Feb-93 | 204 | $48,056 | |
| 9 | A | Heavy Cut | East | | 1-Mar-93 | 213 | $50,032 | |
| 10 | A | Heavy Cut | East | | 1-Apr-93 | 238 | $55,847 | |
| 11 | A | Heavy Cut | East | | 1-May-93 | 226 | $52,997 | |
| 12 | A | Heavy Cut | East | | 1-Jun-93 | 223 | $52,512 | |
| 13 | A | Heavy Cut | West | West | 1-Jan-93 | 225 | $52,891 | |
| 14 | A | Heavy Cut | West | | 1-Feb-93 | 210 | $49,269 | |
| 15 | A | Heavy Cut | West | | 1-Mar-93 | 201 | $47,124 | |
| 16 | A | Heavy Cut | West | | 1-Apr-93 | 237 | $55,783 | |
| 17 | A | Heavy Cut | West | | 1-May-93 | 218 | $51,221 | |
| 18 | A | Heavy Cut | West | | 1-Jun-93 | 230 | $54,051 | |
| 19 | A | Heavy Cut | North | North | 1-Jan-93 | 238 | $55,835 | |
| 20 | A | Heavy Cut | North | | 1-Feb-93 | 242 | $56,781 | |
| 21 | A | Heavy Cut | North | | 1-Mar-93 | 223 | $52,289 | |

**Fig. 8.3** *Use an IF formula to show titles and labels only when they change.*

The formula in cell E7 checks whether the region next to it in D7 is different than the region in the row above. If the regions are different, the adjacent region (D7) appears. If the region above is the same, nothing appears. You don't want column D to show its labels, so you can hide column D.

If you are creating a report that is a summation or cross-tabulation of database information, use the Crosstab ReportWizard. The Crosstab ReportWizard displays subtotals, displays change, and displays break fields more elegantly than through the use of these formulas. If you need to create reports that show all the detail (not summaries), use the formulas in the previous tips rather than the Crosstab ReportWizard.

## Use a formula to increase the line spacing on subtotals

Your reports may look better if you increase the row height for the first row of each record in which the category changes. In figure 8.3, for example, you would probably want to increase the row height in rows 7, 13, and 19. This extra white space makes the groups easy to differentiate.

To increase the row height when the region changes, enter the following formula in cell I7 of figure 8.3:

```
=IF(E7<>"",#N/A,"")
```

Copy this formula down the height of the report. This formula displays the #N/A error in those rows in which a region name appears in column E. Use the Formula Select Special method described in the previous tip, "Use a formula to hide or display rows and columns," to select only the cells containing #N/A. After the cells containing #N/A are selected, you can use the Format Row Height command to increase the height of the rows containing region labels.

# 9

# Printing and Page Layout

Usually the last thing to do is getting your work to fit on a page or getting the right headers and footers to print. When one eye is on the clock and another is on the printer, every tip can help.

## Print only displayed data from an outline

If you attempt to print an outline that has some levels hidden, you may be surprised and aggravated to find that all the levels print. To resolve this problem, you need to let Excel know that you want to use only the visible, selected data. To do this in Excel 4, display the Microsoft Excel 3 tool bar. To the left of the AutoSum button is the Select as Displayed tool. In Excel 4, this tool is also in the Utility category of the Customize tool bars dialog box. You can drag it from there to any tool bar.

To print only the displayed parts of your outline, display the outline as you want it, select the area you want to print, then click the Select as Displayed tool. Now choose the Options Set Print Area command. From there, continue as you would normally print.

## Use the View Manager to save ranges and print settings

 The View Manager is an Excel 4 add-in that saves ranges, as well as displays, and prints settings. If you assign a name to a view, you can return to that view by selecting the name from a list. The print and display settings are saved for each view, so you can assign different view names to different print areas, hidden rows and columns, and page setup settings.

Before you can use the View Manager, it must be added to Excel. If you did not install the View Manager during Excel installation, choose the Options Add-ins command and add the VIEWS.XLA add-in located in the EXCEL\LIBRARY directory. If the VIEWS.XLA file or the LIBRARY directory are not on your computer, reinstall Excel and choose the Custom installation. This will enable you to install the library of add-ins without reinstalling the rest of Excel.

To use the View Manager to make your printing easier:

1. Prepare the worksheet exactly as you want it to print. Hide rows or columns you do not want to print. Select the range to be printed, then choose the Options Set Print Area command.

2. If you will be using the view for other purposes, select from Options Display any settings you want saved. Select the cells or ranges you want selected when the view is displayed.

3. Choose File Page Setup and select the page layout settings that you want the View Manager to save, then choose OK.

4. Choose Window View to display the Views dialog box. Choose the Add button to display the Add View dialog box, type the name you want for the view in the Name edit box.

5. Select the Print Settings check box to save the print settings. If you want to save the hidden rows and columns, select the Hidden Rows & Columns check box. Choose OK.

When you want to return to that view and its associated print area, print settings, and hidden rows and columns, choose Window View. When the Views dialog box appears, select the name of the view you want from the Views list, then choose the Show button. As a shortcut, you can double-click the name of the view in the Views list.

## Use Alt+Enter to create multiple-line headers or footers

 Excel 4 enables you to enter multiple-line headers or footers. To do so:

1. Choose the File Page Setup command. In the Page Setup dialog box that appears, choose the Header or Footer button.

2. The Header dialog box or the Footer dialog box appears. Type your first header or footer line in the left, center, or right section box. When you want to break the line and move to the next line, press Alt+Enter. Continue to type until you need another line, then press Alt+Enter again.

3. Choose OK to return to the Page Setup dialog box. Choose OK a second time to return to Excel.

Use Excel's print preview feature to check that multiple-line headers or footers do not overlap into the body copy area of the page.

## Change the page number code to specify page numbers or print "Page *x* of *xx*"

You can modify a page number in the header or footer to begin printing with any page number you want. You also can add text to the page number, such as *Page 1 of 12*, *Page 2 of 12*, and so on. Display the Header dialog box or the Footer dialog box and click the **Left**, **Center**, or **Right** section box. Position the insertion point where you want the page number to appear. Then specify the page number with one of these methods:

■ To enter a page number that starts with a specific number, click the # icon. This inserts the &P code, which automatically enters page numbers. To increase or decrease a page number from its actual page number, add a number to or subtract a number from the &P code. For example, if you want the first Excel page to print with the page number 31, modify the code to &P+30.

■ To add text to page numbers, type the text (for this example, type **Page**), followed by a space. Click the # icon to insert the &P code. Additionally, you can type another space, the word **of**, and a final space. Then insert the code that prints the total number of pages in the print area by clicking the ++ icon, which inserts the &N code. Your final result would look like Page &P of &N.

## Use the A icon to format headers and footers

Each of the sections in the Header and Footer windows are like miniature notepads. You can format the text in a section by selecting the text and then clicking the *A* icon. This displays a Font dialog box from which you can choose different fonts, sizes, and styles.

## Use one command to remove all page breaks

To remove all manually entered page breaks at once, select the entire worksheet, then choose the Options Remove Page Break command.

To select the entire worksheet with the mouse, click the blank square directly to the left of the column headings. Do not click the dash icon located at the top left of a window.

To select the entire worksheet using the keyboard, first press Shift+Spacebar to select the current row. Then press Ctrl+Spacebar to select columns containing selected cells. (Because all columns now contain a selected cell, all rows and all columns are selected.)

## Repeat vertical and horizontal titles on each page

Repeating titles across the top or down the left side of a multiple-page worksheet can make the printed worksheet easier to use. And when you print a database that is more than one page long, the data on the second page and subsequent pages is easier to read if the database headings are across the top of the page.

To repeat titles or database headings, select the row or rows containing the data you want repeated. Click a row number to select the entire row or press Shift+Spacebar. Then choose the Options Set Print Titles command. When the Set Print Titles dialog box appears, choose OK.

To repeat row headings down the left column, select the column or columns containing the data you want. Select columns by clicking the column headings or select a cell in a column and press Ctrl+Spacebar. Choose the Options Set Print Titles command, then choose OK when the Set Print Titles dialog box appears.

You also can set both horizontal and vertical print titles. Select the rows containing the horizontal headings, then hold down the Ctrl key and click the column headings of the columns containing the left headings. Choose the Options Set Print Titles command, then choose OK from the Set Print Titles dialog box.

## Leave out the titles when selecting a print area

When you select a print area and you are using repeating horizontal or vertical titles like those described in the preceding tip, be careful when you set the print area. If the print area overlaps the print titles, some pages will have two sets of print titles.

To set the print area correctly, select the area you want to print, but do not include the rows or columns used in print titles. Choose the Options Set Print Area command.

## Use F5 to check the current print titles or print area

When you choose the Options commands that set the print area or the print titles, you are assigning a name to those selections. If you want to see the current title or the current print area, press F5 (the Goto key), then select Print_Titles or Print_Area from the list of names. Choose OK, and the current range is selected on the worksheet.

To remove the current print titles or print area, select the entire worksheet and choose the Options Remove Print Titles or Options Remove Print Area command.

## Visually adjust margins and column widths before printing

You may want to check the print preview screen to visually inspect and adjust margins and column widths. This extra step can be worthwhile because what you see on the worksheet may not exactly match what you see on the printout. For example, suppose you have numbers that barely fit in the worksheet cell. If the printed numbers are a little wider than the displayed numbers, they may print as ### because they no longer fit in the cell.

To see a more accurate presentation of printed results and adjust margins or column widths, set your print area, then choose the File Print Preview command. The preview screen is displayed. If the preview is already zoomed so that the text is readable, click the pointer on the preview or choose the Zoom button. This action returns you to viewing the entire preview page. Clicking the preview page or choosing Zoom acts as a toggle between showing the entire page and its layout or showing a readable, magnified view of the page.

With the entire page displayed, check for square black handles that mark page margins or column edges. If you do not see the black handles, choose the Margins button. Use the mouse to drag a margin or column edge handle to a new position. You also can zoom in for a closer view, then drag the margin or column edge. In the zoomed view, you see only the black handles near the edge of the paper, but the pointer changes shape when it is over a column or margin so you will know when you can drag the column or margin. When positioned so that you can drag a column edge or margin, the mouse pointer appears as a two-headed arrow.

**Caution:** Be careful when you move margins or column edges. Your changes also change the worksheet and page setup margin settings. When you change the margins on the page you are viewing, you are also changing the margins on all pages.

## Use File Page Setup to fit your print area to the page

If your printed worksheet or chart *almost* fits on the page, there is an easy solution: just enlarge or reduce the print size. Enlarging or reducing with the File Page Setup command does not affect your worksheet, so you don't have to worry about changing fonts. (It works just like the enlarge or reduce setting on some photocopiers.)

To enlarge or reduce a printed result, choose the File Page Setup command. The Page Setup dialog box appears, with the Reduce/Enlarge to option button and edit box at the bottom of the dialog. Select the option button and type the size you want.

# 10

# Sorting and Databases

There are two advantages to Excel's flat file database capability. First, it serves the nonrelational database needs of many small businesses and corporate departments. Second, it provides analysis and charting of worksheet data that is better than most expensive database packages. In addition, the analysis and charting can be performed without extensive programming. For that reason, many companies download data from their corporate computers into Excel, then use Excel to analyze the data. If you are already familiar with Excel's database, the tips and tools in this chapter will increase your efficiency when using the database and expand the database's capabilities.

## Sort on more than three fields

Although the Sort dialog box shows only three key fields, you can sort on as many database columns or fields as you want. To sort on more than three columns or fields, sort the lowest levels first, working your way up to the highest level.

Suppose that you want to sort column A as the first key, column B as the second key, column C as the third key, and so on for six keys. If Excel had a Sort dialog box that handled six keys at one time, you would need to sort like this:

| Key | 1 | 2 | 3 | 4 | 5 | 6 |
|--------|---|---|---|---|---|---|
| Column | A | B | C | D | E | F |

Excel's Sort dialog box has only three keys, not six, so here is how to sort. You will sort twice. The first sort is on the lowest level columns:

| Key | 1 | 2 | 3 |
|--------|---|---|---|
| Column | D | E | F |

The second time, sort on the higher level columns:

| Key | 1 | 2 | 3 |
|--------|---|---|---|
| Column | A | B | C |

## Set up your database as an island

An Excel database is defined as having field names in one row at the top and data in the rows below. The range of field names and data must have the Database range name. This name is usually defined by selecting all the cells in the database and choosing the **Data Set Database** command. As long as you insert or delete database records (rows) through the middle of this range, the Database name remains intact and usable. If you add data below the last record in the Database range, however, that data is outside the database.

Set up your database so that it appears as an island surrounded on all sides by blank cells. A database set up in this manner is much easier to redefine, as the following tip describes. If you need a second set of titles above your database field names, you can leave a blank row above the field names, type the titles above the blank row, then shrink the row height of the blank row. Your database cannot have completely blank records running through it. That would create a canal, and you would have two database islands, not one.

## Use Ctrl+Shift+* (asterisk) to select a database quickly

 Setting up your database as an island, as described in the preceding tip, enables you to quickly redefine your database if it changes size. After you set your database manually by selecting it and choosing the Data Set Database command, you can quickly rename the database to include any records added at the bottom. This procedure can be recorded with the macro recorder so you can repeat the procedure by pressing a single shortcut key.

If your database has been set up as an island, you can quickly redefine a database that has changed size or shape by following these steps:

1. Press F5 (the Goto key) to display the Goto dialog box.

2. Select the name Database and choose OK.

3. Choose the Formula Select Special command, select the Current Region option, then choose OK. Or simply press Ctrl+Shift+* (asterisk). All cells touching the active cell are selected. This is why you must design the database so that even as it expands, it will be surrounded by a border of blank cells.

4. Choose the Data Set Database command to redefine Database as the newly selected range.

## Automatically define the sort range for your database

Sorting a database is commonplace, but there is no obvious way to do it quickly and easily. You can press F5 (the Goto key), choose the name Database so the database is selected, then sort with the Data Sort command. This causes a problem, however. The field names are included in the Database range, so the field names are sorted with the data. Databases don't work well when field names are in the four hundred and fifty-third record of the database.

You can resolve this problem in Excel 4 by using the OFFSET function to enter a formula that calculates the correct range to be sorted. This formula examines the range named Database and uses that range to define a new name, Sort. The Sort range, however, includes the data but does not include the field names.

The OFFSET formula to use in the Define Name dialog box is

```
=OFFSET(Database,1,0,ROWS(Database)-1)
```

The form for the OFFSET function is

```
OFFSET(Base_Reference,Row_Offset,Col_Offset,Height,Width)
```

The OFFSET function does not move anything on the worksheet. It calculates a new cell or range reference based on another cell or range reference. In this case, you are using the Database range as the *Base_Reference* from which OFFSET can calculate a Sort range.

The arguments used in OFFSET to calculate this new reference follow:

The *Base_Reference* argument in the function is the current Database.

The *Row_Offset* argument of 1 shifts the new Sort reference down one row from where Database is located.

The *Col_Offset* argument of 0 indicates that the new Sort reference is directly in line with the Database range—it is not shifted left or right.

The *Height* argument, ROWS(Database)[min]1, calculates the height of the new Sort reference to be the same height as the Database range, less one row. One row is left out because the range was shifted down one to leave out the field names.

There is no *Width* argument, so the width of the new Sort reference is the same as the width of Database.

To create the Sort name:

1. Choose the Formula Define Name command to display the Define Name dialog box.

2. Type the word **Sort** or any name you want to use in the **Name** edit box.

3. Type the following OFFSET formula in the **Refers To** edit box:

```
=OFFSET(Database,1,0,ROWS(Database)-1)
```

4. Choose OK.

As long as a Database range is defined, you can quickly select its sort range. If you change the Database range, the sort range automatically recalculates before you use it.

To select the sort range:

1. Press the F5 key.

2. The name you typed in the **Name** edit box (**Sort** in the example) will not appear in the **Goto** list. Type that name in the **Reference** edit box.

3. Choose OK.

The Sort range is selected. While the Sort range is selected, you can choose the **Data Sort** command and not worry about sorting field names into the database.

## Use absolute references in database formulas that reference outside cells

If cells in your database contain formulas, make sure that you understand what happens to the formulas when you sort or insert new data. Cell references that refer to other cells in the same record (row) should be relative references (without dollar signs). Cell references that refer to a cell or range outside the database should be absolute references (for example, $B$12). You can create an absolute reference easily by moving the insertion point next to a cell reference in a formula and then pressing the F4 key until the reference includes two dollar signs.

If you use relative references inside a database to refer to cells outside the database, the references change incorrectly when you sort the database, and when you insert or delete records.

## Use a formula to calculate criteria

Most information can be found in a database using simple queries. But some queries are complex and must be calculated. For example, look at the database shown in figure 10.1. What if you wanted to find or extract all records in which the Product is Heavy Cut and the price per unit is less than $235.00? To find those records, your criteria must calculate the unit price for each Heavy Cut record, then find the records where the unit price is less than $235.00.

The trick to using a calculated criterion is to create a new field heading in the Criteria range for calculated criteria. The field name for that calculated criterion *cannot* match any field name that heads the database. In other words, use a made-up field name for a calculated criterion. You cannot put a calculated criterion under a valid field name in the Criteria range.

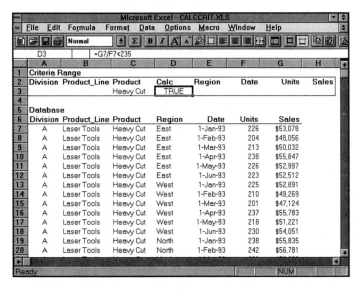

**Fig. 10.1** *Use a dummy field name above calculated criterion.*

The rule for creating a formula for your calculated criterion is that the result of the calculation should be TRUE or FALSE. The cell being tested must be in the top row of data. For example, if the first row of data is row 12 and you want to test column B, your formula should test B12.

Calculated criteria that result in TRUE are found or extracted by a database command. Database functions (Dfunctions) analyze the records that meet calculated criteria that result in TRUE. This is easiest to do if you build formulas that test for equalities: is one side equal to the other, is one side less than the other, and so on. Here are some examples of calculated criteria:

| Criterion | Explanation |
|-----------|-------------|
| =D12=G12 | Checks for an exact match between data in the same record. Tests TRUE when the cells in column D of a record are the same as the cells in column G of the same record. TRUE results are found or extracted. |
| =B12=B13 | Checks for an exact match between data in two adjacent records. Tests TRUE when two adjacent records have the same data in column B. |
| =C12<D12/2 | Checks for records in which C12 is less than half of D12. |
| =C12>$B$12 | Checks for records in which the data in column C is greater than a number typed in cell B12. B12 is outside the database. |

In figure 10.1, the criteria to find records in which the Product is Heavy Cut and the price per unit is less than $235.00 are entered in the Criteria range. Notice that the heading Calc is used above the calculated criterion. (You can use any word that is not a valid field name above a calculated criterion.) Check the Criteria range by selecting it with the F5 key to make sure that any calculated criterion heading is within the Criteria range. The calculation used for the criterion is

=G7/F7<235

## Use calculated criteria to find blank or filled cells in a database

Use calculated criteria like those described in the preceding tip when you need to find records that contain a blank or find records that contain only filled data. For example, in the database and criterion shown in figure 10.1, you can find blank cells in column C by entering the following calculated criterion in cell D3 of the Criteria range:

```
=C7=" "
```

Notice that this cell is under the Calc dummy field heading. If you want to find records that contain only filled cells in column C, use a calculated criterion such as

```
=C7<>" "
```

## Extract database data to another worksheet when creating reports

To create a report from the data in a database, first extract the data to a separate worksheet and format it there. This way has several advantages:

- You can have only one Extract range at a time on the worksheet containing the database. If you extract to a separate worksheet, however, you can have multiple worksheets, each with their own Criteria and Extract range, based on the original Database.

- With a single report on each worksheet, you don't have to worry about the row and column formatting from one report interfering with the formatting of another report.

- You can view multiple extracted reports at the same time by arranging the separate worksheets.

- Each worksheet that contains an extracted report can be saved as a separate file for use in E-mail, printing, and so on, or can be turned into its own database file.

The following instructions are terse if you have never performed a database extract. Before attempting this extract, you may want to learn about a normal database extract. (The best-selling Que book, *Using Excel 4 for Windows*, Special Edition, contains explanations and examples of extracting.)

To extract data from a database on one worksheet to an Extract range on another worksheet:

1. Create a worksheet that contains a database meeting all the Excel database rules. Make sure that you name the database by selecting it and choosing the Data Set Database command. Save the database worksheet to a file name that you do not plan to change.

2. Create a second worksheet to contain the extract report. In this worksheet, you must create a valid Criteria range and Extract range. Use the appropriate field names from the Database range on the other worksheet. Select the Criteria range and choose the Data Set Criteria command. Select the Extract headings and choose the Data Set Extract command.

   You have now created and named a Database on one worksheet and created and named a Criteria and Extract range on a different worksheet.

3. Activate the worksheet containing the Extract range.

4. Choose the Formula Define Name command.

5. The Define Name dialog box appears. Type the name **Database** in the Name edit box.

6. Type the following formula in the **Refers to** edit box:

   =*filename*.XLS!Database

where *filename* is the name of the worksheet containing the Database range.

7. Choose OK.

Figure 10.2 shows you how the light machinery database appears while an external extract is being set up on the XCPTRPRT.XLS worksheet.

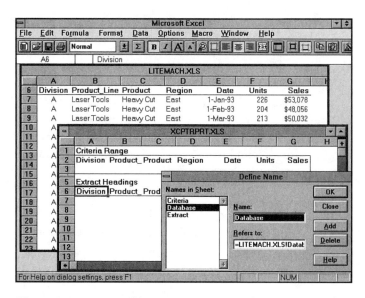

**Fig. 10.2**  *Extract data to a separate worksheet to make reports easier to create.*

When you are ready to create your report, make sure that both files are open. Then follow these steps:

1. Activate the worksheet containing the Extract range.

2. Enter any criteria in the Criteria range to limit the data extracted.

3. Choose the Data Extract command. Select the Unique Records Only check box if you want to

remove records where all extracted fields contain the same data.

4. Choose OK or press Enter.

Extracted data that matches your criteria is copied from the worksheet containing the database and put below the Extract headings.

## Use the extract feature to check for misspelled entries

You can check for misspelled data in your database by doing a unique extract on the field you suspect contains misspellings. Suppose that your database contains twenty different product names entered under the field name Product. Because the data was entered manually, some product names could be misspelled, which would invalidate searches, sorts, and analysis.

To check a column for misspelled words, you must create a one-field Extract range for the field you want to check and do a unique extract. If there are only twenty or thirty valid entries, it's easy to see incorrect entries. For example, if you suspect data under the Product heading is misspelled:

1. Create a Database range and a Criteria range as you would to extract data. Make sure that the Criteria range is clear of criteria.

2. Select a cell that has nothing below it for as far as the bottom of the worksheet.

3. Type **Product** (the field heading) into the cell.

4. Select the cell and choose the **Data Set Extract** command.

5. Choose the Data Extract command.

6. Select the Unique Records Only check box.

7. Choose OK.

The cells under Product fill with a list containing each unique word in the Product field. There will be no duplicates.

Look through this list for misspelled product names. If you find a misspelled product name, you can find its location in the database as follows:

1. Choose the Formula Find command.

2. Type into the Find What edit box the word as it is misspelled.

3. Select the Look in Values option and choose OK.

4. When you find and correct the misspelling, press the F7 key to repeat the Find command. This ensures that no other words have the same misspelling.

# 11

## CHAPTER

# Creating Charts

If you've been an accountant or chief financial officer for forty years, you can probably scan a page of numbers and pick out some obscure trend. The rest of us, however, are better served looking for visual changes—something our hunter-and-gatherer ancestors did for a few hundred thousand years. It's just plain easier to find important changes or relationships when you look at a chart.

### Use the ChartWizard to flip the chart axis

Excel's automatic charting rule tells it that a data series (a line of data in a line chart) is the data that goes the long way in the cells you selected. For example, if you selected a range of data whose width is greater than its height, Excel assumes the data series goes across the row. (A line in a line chart would connect all the numbers in the same row.)

Sometimes, the data you select is not the way Excel expects it, and the resulting chart appears sideways—what you wanted on the horizontal axis is on the vertical axis, and vice versa. You can correct this problem easily with the ChartWizard:

1. Activate the worksheet containing the chart data.

2. Activate the chart. If the chart is embedded in the worksheet, double-click it.

3. Click the ChartWizard tool at the right side of the standard toolbar. This action displays a Wizard window that enables you to select a different range.

4. Choose the Next button.

5. Note the two option buttons labeled Data Series in Rows and Data Series in Columns. Select the opposite of the current button. The sample chart changes to show the new orientation.

6. Choose OK.

## Use chart templates for frequently drawn charts

If you frequently create the same custom chart but use different data, you should learn about chart templates. A chart template is a blank chart that stores all the formats and settings for a chart. All you add is data, and the chart redraws using the new data.

To create a chart template:

1. Create a chart exactly like the one you want to repeat. Set the chart's patterns, colors, legend location, fixed titles, axis scaling, page setup settings, and other formatting.

2. Choose File Save As.

3. Type a name for the chart in the File Name edit box. Indicate in the file name the type of template it is, for example, CBUDGET.XLT. (The *C* stands for *chart*.) Otherwise, you cannot tell the difference between a chart template and a worksheet template.

4. Choose Template from the Save File as Type pull-down list.

5. Select the EXCEL\XLSTART directory.

6. Choose OK.

The next time you start Excel, choose the File New command to see the chart template listed among the other types of templates. To create a chart using the template's formatting:

1. Select the data you want to chart.

2. Choose the File New command.

3. Instead of selecting Chart to open a new chart, select the name of your template.

4. Choose OK.

Excel opens your template, gives it a new name, and displays the selected data in the format defined by the template.

## Avoid the Gallery menu to preserve chart formatting

If you create a chart and customize it with colors, patterns, custom scales, and so on, be careful if you must change the type of chart. Do not change a customized chart (for example, a customized bar chart to a column chart) using the Gallery menu. If you do so, you may lose your custom formatting.

To change chart types and preserve formatting:

1. Choose the Format Main Chart command.

2. The Format Chart dialog box appears. Select a new chart type from the Main Chart Type pull-down list.

3. Small samples of the types of charts are displayed. Select the type of chart from the Data View group.

4. Choose OK.

## Ctrl+click to select a single data point on a chart

If you click a line, bar, or column, all the markers in the series are selected. Usually that's okay because you want to format an entire series in the same way. If you want a different color or pattern for a single line, bar, or column, however, you need to know how to select it.

To select a single marker, hold down the Ctrl key as you click the marker, bar, or column. Notice that the selection handle appears on only the marker you clicked.

## Drag a pie chart wedge to emphasize it

If you want pie chart segments to separate so that a certain segment stands out, just click the segment and drag it away from the center. As you drag the wedge out, the pie shrinks. You do not need to drag a wedge very far to make it stand out.

## Create line chart symbols

You can create line chart symbols in Paintbrush and use them as the symbols for an entire line or a single data point. This is helpful for charts, especially those used for overhead transparencies, in which the line chart symbols provided by Excel are too small. You can also create special symbols that your industry or company uses.

To create a line chart symbol:

1. First create and save your line chart.

2. Switch to the Program Manager and start Paint-brush, the bit-map drawing program in the Accessories group.

3. Draw and color the symbol. Some experimenting may be required to size the symbol correctly. You may want to create a Paintbrush file of the custom symbols you use frequently.

4. After you draw the symbol in Paintbrush, click one of the two select tools at the top of the Paintbrush toolbar.

5. Select the symbol by dragging around it, then choose the **Edit Copy** command.

6. Switch to Excel and select your chart.

7. If you want to use your symbol for every data point on a line, click the chart line. If you want to use your symbol to mark a single data point on a line, Ctrl+click that data point.

8. Choose the **Edit Paste** command. Your symbol replaces the selected markers on the line.

## Format the value axis

The value axis, also referred to as the Y or vertical axis in two-dimensional charts, takes its format from the first numeric cell of the first data series. Change the format of that cell in the worksheet if you want to change the numeric format of the axis.

## Make legend titles with multiple lines

If your legends look awkward because the titles are too long, you can correct them by making the titles wrap to a second line. The trick is to realize that you cannot enter the line break character, Alt+Enter, in a legend title. But you can enter a line break in a worksheet cell, then link the legend title to that cell.

To break a legend title into two lines:

1. Select the worksheet cell that contains the legend title you want to split.

2. Move the insertion point in the formula bar to where you want the legend title broken.

3. Press Alt+Enter. A black vertical character appears in the worksheet cell.

4. Press Enter to reenter the text in the cell.

5. Activate the chart.

As you can see, the legend's title has split at the point in the text where you pressed Alt+Enter. If you do not want to mar the headings in your worksheet with the black mark of a line break character, you can break the legend title into two lines as follows:

1. Create another split title in a cell in an unobtrusive part of the worksheet.

2. Activate the chart sheet.

3. Choose the **Chart Edit Series** command.

4. The Edit Series dialog box appears. Select the series you want the title for, then clear the Name edit box.

5. Activate the worksheet containing the imposter title. (You can activate a worksheet and click in its cells while the Name edit box is selected.)

6. Click the cell containing the imposter title.

7. Choose OK to accept the new name for that data series.

## Link worksheet numbers or text to a floating text block

Some charts are more informative when they show dates, numbers, titles, or comments linked to cells on the worksheet. This procedure can be useful if you always want to show the current date in a chart or if you want a text comment from a worksheet cell to show up in the chart as a floating text block. And when the dates, numbers, titles, or comments change in the worksheet, they change in the chart, too.

To link a floating text block in a chart to the data in a worksheet cell:

1. Click a blank area of the chart so that no text is selected.

2. Type an equal sign.

3. Activate the worksheet that has the cell you want to link. You can activate the worksheet by clicking it, choosing it from the Window menu, or pressing Ctrl+F6.

4. Click the cell that contains the data you want in the chart.

5. Press Enter.

The chart reactivates and shows the contents of the worksheet cell in a floating text block. You can format this text block like any floating text.

If you select the floating text that is linked and look in the formula bar, you can see that you created an external reference formula to the worksheet cell. This formula is like the formulas used to link worksheet cells.

## Use the ChartWizard to expand charted data

If the data plotted by your chart has expanded to include more worksheet cells, you don't need to draw a new chart. You can use the ChartWizard to extend the data range. Follow these steps:

1. Activate the worksheet containing the data.

2. Activate the chart. Double-click the chart if it is embedded.

3. Click the ChartWizard tool at the far right side of the standard toolbar. This action displays the first Wizard window. The edit box in this window enables you to edit the ranges used by charts.

4. Edit the range in the Range edit box, or enter a new data range by selecting the cell reference you want to change and clicking or dragging the cell in the worksheet.

5. Choose the Next button.

6. Choose OK.

## Name data ranges to expand or contract charts

 In many sales and budget worksheets, you must add the new data for each month to the end of the existing data. However, if there is a chart of this data, the chart does not automatically expand to include the new month's data.

You have a few less-than-optimal solutions. You can create the chart so that it includes the worksheet range that the data will eventually occupy. But if you plan for twelve months of data and it is March, for example, the chart has nine months of blank space. Another alternative is to edit the chart's series formulas to include the additional cells. You can use the Chart Edit Series command or click the ChartWizard to reselect or extend the range of cells charted. But this procedure is tedious, prone to error, and takes a lot of time because it must be performed every month.

Often a better solution is to edit your chart so that it looks for its data in named ranges on the worksheet. If you change the definition of the name, the chart automatically expands or contracts to include the data in the new name.

Figure 11.1 shows a worksheet with data through April for two data series, Revenue and Cost. Notice that cell A3 contains X_Titles, a text title that is normally not there. It is used later to create names more easily. If you want to hide the title, format its font color or use the custom numeric format of four semicolons (; ; ; ;). To enter this custom numeric format:

1. Choose the Format Number command.

2. Type ;;;; in the Code edit box.

3. Choose OK.

This custom format hides all numbers and text. After it is entered, you can reuse it. The custom format will appear at the bottom of the Format Codes list in All Categories.

To re-create this example:

1. Type the data as shown in figure 11.1.

2. Select a cell in the data.

3. Press Ctrl+Shift+* (asterisk) on the typing keys to select all the data.

4. Press F11 to create the chart. You can also choose the File New command and select Chart.

5. Use the Window Arrange command to arrange the windows horizontally.

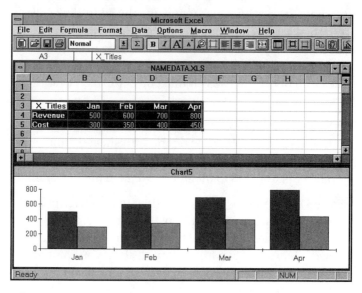

**Fig. 11.1** *Use the labels in A3:A5 to name data ranges for the chart.*

To see how the chart does not update automatically, type entries for May: a title and amounts for May's revenue and cost. Notice that the chart does not reflect the data you appended. Erase the May title and data.

To edit the chart so that it expands to include monthly data added to the end, you must create names on the worksheet, then edit these names into the chart's series formulas. First, create the names on the worksheet that describe where the data and the category (X-axis) labels are located:

1. Select cells A3:E5. Notice that cells A3, A4, and A5 contain text that can be used as a name to identify the data to the right. The following command uses the text in the leftmost cell to assign a name to the data cells to the right.

2. Choose the Formula Create Names command.

3. The Create Names dialog box appears. Select the Left Column check box. Make sure that all other check boxes are cleared.

4. Choose OK or press Enter.

You can check whether the three names for the cells from B3:E5 have been created correctly by pressing the Goto key, F5. Select the X_Titles, Revenue, or Cost name from the list and choose OK. The labels or data in cells B3:E5 are selected. The text in column A is not included.

Now you use the Edit Series command to edit the chart's series formulas so the chart looks for named ranges rather than specific cell references. To edit the chart's series formulas:

1. Activate the chart.

2. Choose the Chart Edit Series command. The Edit Series dialog box appears. Figure 11.2 shows this dialog box with the Revenue data series selected. Notice that the edit boxes show you which cells are used to retrieve a series name (legend), X labels (horizontal axis), and Y values (vertical axis).

3. Select the first data series, Revenue, from the Series list box. The edit boxes on the right show the cells that this series refers to.

4. Edit the X Labels edit box so it uses the range name X_Titles instead of $B$3:$E$3.

5. Edit the Y Values edit box so it uses the range name Revenue instead of $B$4:$E$4.

6. Choose the **Define** button. The edited Revenue series should appear as shown in figure 11.3.

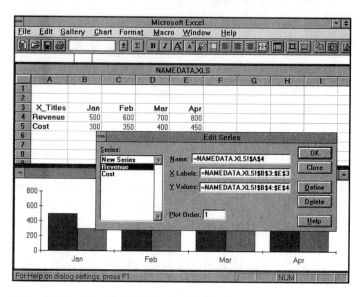

**Fig. 11.2** *Use the Edit Series dialog box to see the worksheet cells that the chart references.*

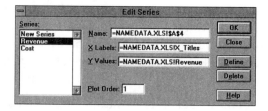

**Fig. 11.3** *Replace the cell references with named ranges on the worksheet.*

7. Repeat steps 3 through 6 for the Cost series. In step 5, use the range name Cost to replace $B$5:$E$5.

8. Choose OK or press Enter.

9. Save your chart.

The chart now looks to named ranges on the worksheet to get its data. If the named ranges are redefined to include more or less data, the chart adjusts automatically.

To see how the chart adjusts:

1. Add a title and data for the month of May in F3:F5.

2. Reselect the range of all chart data, A3:F5.

3. Choose the Formula Create Names command and select only the Left Column check box. Clear all other check boxes.

4. Choose OK. You are prompted whether you want to redefine each of the names. Choose the Yes button each time.

When all the names are redefined, the chart is redrawn to include the new data defined by the new range names. To make this process even easier, you can use a recorded macro to automate updating the data and renaming the chart data.

## Name formulas to adjust charts with changing amounts of data

If you are a developer who creates Excel 4 applications for use by others, you may want to take the previous tip one step further. With the use of named formulas, you can make charts that automatically adjust when the user appends a new month of data. The user does not even have to redefine the names. In this method, formulas recalculate the definition of the name and do all the work behind the scenes. The entire process is accomplished without a macro.

To use this technique, you must go through the process described in the preceding tip. The chart references for **X** Labels and **Y** Values in the Edit Series dialog box must be replaced with names that refer to the worksheet.

This technique creates names in the worksheet that are formulas. These formulas calculate the cell or range reference that defines the named range. When you change the size of a data series by appending data for a new month or removing a month, the formula recalculates and produces a new reference for the range.

To make this work:

1. Create the worksheet and chart described in the preceding tip. The chart must reference the names in the worksheet.

2. Activate the worksheet.

3. Choose the Formula **Define Name** command.

4. The Define Name dialog box appears. Select one of the names referenced by the chart (for example, Revenue).

5. Select the **Refers To** edit box. Press the F2 key so you can edit in this box without changing the references. Notice that when you press F2, the Status bar changes from Enter to Edit.

6. Enter the following formulas in the **Refers to** edit box for each of the range names used by the chart (see fig. 11.4). Choose the **Add** button after typing each formula:

| Name | Formula |
| --- | --- |
| X_Titles | =OFFSET($B$3,0,0,1,COUNTA($B$3:$M$3)) |
| Revenue | =OFFSET($B$4,0,0,1,COUNTA($B$4:$M$4)) |
| Cost | =OFFSET($B$5,0,0,1,COUNTA($B$5:$M$5)) |

7. Choose OK or press Enter.

**Fig. 11.4** *Use formulas to create names that update charts.*

You have just created named formulas. In this example, the OFFSET functions calculate a range that defines each name. Data typed into the first blank cell at the end of a row of data increases the COUNTA result by one. This action increases the width of the named range by one.

The OFFSET function is useful in worksheets and invaluable in macros. The form for the OFFSET function is

`OFFSET(Base_Point,Row_Offset,Col_Offset,Height,Width)`

In the Revenue example, the *base_point*, or where the Revenue range begins, is $B$4. The first data point is not offset by any rows or columns from $B$4, so the *row_offset* and the *col_offset* are both zero. The *height* of the data range you are defining is one cell high. The *width* is defined by how many adjacent cells are filled between $B$4 and the cell for the last month, $M$4.

You must know one last thing before you can start adding data to the end of a series. The chart may not always update when you type new data at the end of the series because the chart doesn't recognize the data. To correct this problem manually, you can change one of the numbers in the chart's data series. This forces the chart to reexamine its worksheet references, and the chart will update and include the new data.

If you want the update to always be automatic, type
=**NOW**( ) in a worksheet cell. The NOW function results in
the current date and time. Next, you must link the chart to
the cell containing the NOW function:

1. Activate the chart.

2. Click a blank area and type an equal sign to start a
   formula in the formula bar of the chart.

3. Activate the worksheet.

4. Click the cell containing the NOW function, then
   press Enter.

Because NOW is always changing, the chart reevaluates its
references and in the process, recalculates the names defined by the OFFSET formulas. If you do not want the date
from the NOW function to show in the chart, format it the
same color as the chart background so that it can't be
seen.

## Use the Edit Series command to retitle legends

When you create legends with the ChartWizard or choose
the Chart Add Legend command, Excel uses the labels
from each data series to create titles for the legend. If your
chart does not have labels for a legend or you want to
change the legends, use the Chart Edit Series command to
create or edit legend labels.

To change the titles used in legends:

1. Add a legend to the chart, if it does not have one, by
   choosing the Chart Add Legend command.

2. Choose the Chart Edit Series command.

3. The Edit Series dialog box appears. Select from the Series list the name of the data series that has the legend title you want to change.

4. Select the entire contents of the Name edit box. The Name edit box displays the cell from which the legend is getting its title for this data series.

5. You have two choices: link the legend title in the Name edit box or type a new one.

   If you want to link the legend title for the data series to a different worksheet cell, choose the Window menu and select the worksheet containing the cell with the new legend title. Scroll to and select the cell containing the new title. The external reference to that new title appears in the Name edit box.

   If you want to type in a legend title and not use one in a worksheet cell, clear the Name edit box and type the title you want. This new title will not change if you change the label for the data in the worksheet.

6. Choose OK.

## Change the palette to adjust the color in 3-D surface maps

The colors for 3-D surface maps come from the color palette. They cannot be changed by formatting, as you would change colors or patterns in other charts. To change the colors in a 3-D surface map:

1. Activate the worksheet from which the chart was created.

2. Choose the Options Color Palette command.

3. Select the color you want to change from the colors in the Color Palette group.

4. Choose the Edit button.

5. The Color Picker window appears. Select a custom color from this window.

6. Choose OK.

7. The custom color you selected replaces the color in the Color Palette group. The custom color you selected replaces the color selected in step 3 throughout the worksheet as well as in the chart.

8. Choose OK to accept this new color palette.

## Use the Gallery Combination command to display two chart scales

You can create charts that have two scales—one on the left and another on the right—by choosing the Gallery Combination command. From the Chart Gallery dialog box, select the two-axis chart that is closest to the chart you want, and choose OK.

If you want to change the type of chart used by the master chart, the one with the left axis, choose the Format Main Chart command. If you want to change the type of chart used by the right axis, choose the Format Overlay command. In either case, select a new chart type from the Main Chart Type pull-down list, then select a specific chart from the Data View group.

# 12

# Creating Macros

Excel's macro language can be used by novices or application developers. The novice can record and modify macros. The application developer can create macros using Excel's programming language, which contains more than 1000 functions.

## Understand how Excel macros are displayed

Excel macros are displayed in a way that is different than other macros or programming languages. This concept is best understood by comparing Excel macros with Excel formulas.

The worksheet displays a formula's *result*. If you press Ctrl+' (the backward apostrophe on the ~ key), the display switches so that you can see the worksheet's formula.

With an Excel macro, however, the macro function and formula are displayed. The results of the macro are hidden. If you display a macro sheet and press Ctrl+' (backward apostrophe), you will see the results produced by macro functions. These results may appear as TRUE,

FALSE, an error value, or a calculated or an entered result
that is a number or text, as follows:

| Result | Produced |
|---|---|
| TRUE | When a function operates correctly |
| FALSE | When the function operates but does not produce a result, or when you choose the Cancel button in a dialog box displayed by a function |
| Calculation | When a formula calculates a result |
| Data entered | When the user enters data in the Input dialog box |
| #Error | When a function is used incorrectly or when one or more arguments are incorrect |

## Use uppercase for macros to preserve built-in hot keys

Excel 4 contains built-in shortcut keys such as Ctrl+b for
bold and Ctrl+i for italic. If you create a macro that uses
a lowercase shortcut key combination, your macro has
precedence over the built-in key when the macro sheet
is open. Preserve the built-in shortcut keys by using uppercase letters with your shortcut keys. For example,
use Ctrl+Shift+B if you want to preserve the built-in bold
shortcut of Ctrl+b.

**Note:** As you know, you must press Shift to produce an
uppercase letter. This book "spells it out" by writing, for
example, Ctrl+Shift+B rather than Ctrl+B.

## Type formulas, functions, and range names in lowercase

Excel macro sheets and worksheets check cell references,
functions, and range names when you enter them. If your

entry is valid, Excel capitalizes it. Function names and references are changed to all uppercase. Range names are capitalized to match the way they were typed when the name was created. For this reason, it is a good idea to create range names with a leading capital letter.

If Excel does not change the capitalization of a function, cell reference, or range name on entry, Excel does not recognize the entry as valid. By always typing your formulas, functions, and range names in lowercase, you can recognize errors because they remain in lowercase after the formula is entered.

## Disable STEP functions but keep them available for later troubleshooting

The STEP function is a handy function to insert before any section of macro code you want to examine. The macro runs normally until it reaches the STEP function, where it then runs in Step mode. While in Step mode, you can choose the Evaluate button to see the partial and full results from a function or choose the Continue button to return to normal run mode.

After your macro is finished, you may want to remove the STEP functions because they get in the way of normal operation. Rather than clear the STEP functions, however, deactivate them and keep them in the macro. If you must troubleshoot the macro later, you can reactivate the STEP functions you used during development.

To deactivate the operational STEP functions:

1. Select the areas containing STEPs you want to deactivate.

2. Choose the Formula Replace command.

3. Type =STEP in the Find What edit box. Type STEP in the Replace With edit box.

4. Choose the Replace All button. This action replaces all =STEP entries with STEP. Without the equal sign, the entry is text and is not evaluated by the macro.

You can reactivate the STEP function to troubleshoot a macro you thought was performing correctly. Select the macro code that is questionable, then use the Formula Replace command to replace all occurrences of STEP with =STEP.

## Disable a section of a macro when debugging

Sometimes while debugging a macro, you must momentarily disable a section of macro code. To do so:

1. Select the cells containing the functions you want to disable.

2. Choose the Formula Replace command.

3. Type = in the Find What edit box. Type **eql** in the Replace With edit box.

4. Choose the Replace All button. This changes the code to text that is ignored.

To make the code operational, reverse the process. Select the same cells. Use the Formula Replace command to replace the text eql with = in the macro.

## Pause recorded dialog boxes so you can make selections

When you replay a recorded macro, the dialog boxes in which you make selections never appear, so you cannot change their options. It is very easy to make the dialog boxes display so you can select new options during the macro playback.

To display any recorded dialog box, first find the macro function for that dialog box. These functions are somewhat obvious. For example, FORMAT.FONT displays the Font dialog box and ALIGNMENT displays the text Alignment dialog box. Make the dialog box display by typing a question mark in front of the first parenthesis. For example:

```
=ALIGNMENT?(1,FALSE,3,0)
```

When you run the macro, the Alignment dialog box is displayed and waits for you to choose the OK button. The dialog box options you selected when you recorded the macro are stored as the arguments of the function and are used as the default settings for the dialog box when it is displayed.

## Use the FORMULA INPUT combination for simple data entry

Many people want to use macros for data entry. Following is an easy way to make a simple data entry macro that prompts the operator, checks the type of data (text or number), and enters the data in the correct cell. To create this macro:

1. Make sure that your worksheet is active. Choose the Macro Record command.

2. The Record Macro dialog box appears. Type a name for the macro, but do not use spaces. Enter a shortcut key if you want. Choose OK.

3. Choose the Macro menu. If the command Relative Record is available, press Esc so the Relative Record command remains unchanged. If the command Absolute Record is available, choose it.

   The recorder records the absolute cell locations where you want to enter data. The macro works on playback no matter which cell you start it from. (Macros recorded in Relative Record mode select cells relative to the starting location when played back.)

4. Select the first cell in which you want to enter data.

5. Type a description of the data that goes in the cell, then press Enter. The description is recorded in the macro, and helps you identify which cell the macro is entering data into.

6. Repeat steps 4 and 5 for each cell and description. Select the cells in the order in which you want the operator to enter the data. If you make a mistake, just continue. Later, you can edit the mistake in the macro sheet.

7. Choose the Macro Stop Recorder command.

This process creates a macro that selects each data entry cell and enters a description in that cell. If you choose the Macro Run command, select the name of your macro, and choose OK, you see the macro repeat your selections and entries.

To modify your macro so it prompts an operator for the data to enter:

1. Choose the Window command and activate the macro sheet containing the macro you named. The macro's name appears in row 1. The macro code appears as SELECT functions that select cells using the row and column number and also FORMULA functions that enter the description in the selected cell. You will modify the FORMULA function so it displays a dialog box that prompts the operator for an entry. The macro code will look similar to

```
=SELECT("R3C3")
=FORMULA("Amount")
```

2. Select the quoted text inside the FORMULA function (including the quotation marks) and choose the Formula Paste Function command.

3. The Paste Function dialog box appears. Select the INPUT function from the Paste Function list. Make sure that the Paste Arguments check box is selected, then choose OK.

    The FORMULA function cell now looks like

    ```
    =FORMULA(INPUT(message_text,type_num,title_text,default,
        x_pos,y_pos,help_ref))
    ```

4. Replace *message_text* with a message that prompts the operator. Enclose the message in quotation marks. This message will appear in the dialog box.

5. Replace *type_num* with 1 if you want to restrict entries to numbers or dates or 2 if entries can be text, numbers, or dates.

6. Replace *title_text* with the title you want to appear at the top of the dialog box. Enclose the title in quotation marks.

7. Replace *default* with any number or text you want the operator to use as the standard entry. If *type_num* is 2 (text), you must enclose your text default in quotation marks.

8. Delete the *x_pos, y_pos,* and *help_ref* arguments.

9. Press Enter.

Here's an example FORMULA INPUT combination:

```
=FORMULA(INPUT("Type the amount.",1,"Expense Entry",20))
```

Repeat this process for a few FORMULA functions. Then *activate the appropriate worksheet* and run your macro.

If your macro does not run, check to make sure that there are matching quotation marks and matching parentheses. There should be no spaces outside quoted text. Make sure that the commas are in the correct locations and that you typed commas, not periods. Make sure that the worksheet is active when you run this macro; otherwise, it may enter data on top of the macro code.

## Use FORMULA and COPY to transfer data between worksheets

People who record macros are accustomed to transferring blocks of data by copying from one worksheet, activating another worksheet, and pasting into that sheet. This method was slow due to the process of activating worksheets and using the Clipboard. Another frequently used method was to build a FOR-NEXT or FOR-CELL loop that went through every cell in the block, and use the FORMULA function to transfer the cells one at a time. This method was usually faster because the receiving worksheet did not need to be activated. The macro could also calculate or manipulate the data as it was being transferred.

With Excel 4, you can transfer blocks of data rapidly. Neither the source nor target worksheet needs to be active, but they must be open. To transfer the data, you use the COPY function:

```
COPY(from_reference,to_reference)
```

The *from_reference* and *to_reference* arguments must meet the same cell size and shape conditions used when manually copying and pasting. If you must perform calculations with the data in *from_reference* as it is being transferred, you should still use a loop and the FORMULA function. (This method is described in the next tip.)

## Use **FORMULA** to calculate data as it transfers

The FORMULA command is used to transfer data from one location to another. Its form is

```
FORMULA(reference_from,reference_to)
```

If the *reference_to* argument is not specified, FORMULA puts the values from *reference_from* into the active cell. Most macro programmers are accustomed to using FORMULA by specifying a *from* location and a *to* location to transfer data between open worksheets. For example:

```
=FORMULA(BUDGET.XLS!$A$6,SUMMARY.XLS!June)
```

This transfers the amount from $A$6 in the BUDGET.XLS worksheet to the cell named June in the SUMMARY.XLS worksheet. You can do calculations during the transfer. Consider these two examples:

```
=FORMULA(BUDGET.XLS!$A$6*9,SUMMARY.XLS!June)
```

```
=FORMULA(JUNE.XLS!Amount+JULY.XLS!Amount,SUMMARY.XLS!Total)
```

The first example multiplies the value from $A$6 times 9, then transfers it. The second example adds the numbers stored in the name Amount from two worksheets, then transfers that sum to the cell named Total on the SUMMARY.XLS worksheet.

## Use the **STRUCTM.XLT** macro to indent macro code

Excel comes with a template that can make your macro code more readable. It indents interior portions of FOR-NEXT and WHILE-NEXT loops and conditional sections under a block IF. To make this feature available:

1. Open the STRUCTM.XLT macro, which is in the \EXCEL\EXAMPLES directory.

2. In the macro, select all the cells that contain block IF functions, FOR loops, and WHILE loops.

3. Press Ctrl+n to indent or Ctrl+m to remove the indent. The macro automatically recognizes which functions should be indented.

## Use Open EIS Pak to develop information system applications quickly

If you develop applications using Excel, you should look into Microsoft Open EIS Pak—an Excel add-in that is a menu-driven toolkit for beginning to advanced macro programmers. It helps you create opening screens, custom menus, and screens containing tables and charts. You can add to your application buttons or commands that query databases or SQL servers, build cross-tabulations, or display detailed data when the user double-clicks a summary.

Macro writers of all levels can attach their recorded or programmed macros to the application that Open EIS Pak produces. You can purchase the Open EIS Pak for $99 directly from Microsoft by calling 800-426-9400.

## Use authoring software to develop help files quickly

In addition to creating Excel menus and dialog boxes, you can also create custom help files that are called from those menus and dialog boxes. Custom help files can use all the features available in the Windows help engine. The capabilities you see in Excel help files—including searches, jumps, and pop-up definitions—can be added to your custom help files.

To create a custom help file, you write a document in Word for Windows, insert codes in that document, then compile the document using a help compiler available from Microsoft. When performed manually, the process is, at best, tedious.

If you want to develop professional-looking printed documentation and convert that documentation to on-line help that can be used by Excel, Word for Windows, or Access, you should use Doc-To-Help. Doc-To-Help is a Word for Windows 2 utility that gives you document templates containing the styles, macros, and tables to produce good-looking printed documentation.

Using custom menus and tools added to Word by Doc-To-Help, you can mark your documentation for items to be used as jump points, index items, pop-up definitions, and so on. Doc-To-Help then converts your Word for Windows 2 file to a help file you can use with your custom Windows applications and macros. For information about Doc-To-Help, contact

> WexTech Systems, Inc.
> 310 Madison Avenue, Suite 905
> New York, NY  10017
> 212-949-9595

## Turn graphic objects or drawings into buttons

You can turn any graphic object or drawing into a button that runs a macro. To assign a macro to a graphic, a drawing, or even an embedded chart:

1.  Open the macro sheet containing the macro you want to run.

2.  Activate the worksheet containing the graphic object you want want to link a macro to.

3.  Select the graphic, drawing, or chart. Black handles appear at its corners when it is selected.

4. Choose the Macro Assign to Object command.

5. The Assign To Object dialog box appears. Select from the Assign Macro list the macro you want to run, then choose OK.

6. Select a cell so that the graphic object is not selected.

Clicking the graphic object runs the macro. If you need to see which macro is assigned to a button, hold down the Ctrl key as you click a button, then choose the Macro Assign to Object command. The assigned macro appears in the Reference edit box.

## Use Ctrl+click to select custom buttons

After you draw a graphic and assign a macro to it, you may need to move or reformat the graphic. Each time you click the graphic to select it for formatting, however, the graphic runs the macro assigned to it. To move or reformat a graphic or button that has a macro assigned to it, hold down the Ctrl key and click the graphic or button.

## Split windows to keep buttons in view

If you use macro buttons to run macros, you may find that the buttons move out of sight when you scroll the window. To prevent this:

1. Place buttons along the top or left side of the worksheet.

2. Select the cell that is below the row of buttons and to the right of the column of buttons.

3. Choose the Window Freeze Pane command. This freezes the top rows and left columns. The top row

stays in place as you scroll up or down, and the left columns stay in place as you scroll left or right.

4. When you want to remove the split panes from the active window, choose the **W**indow Unfreeze Panes command.

## Assign your macros to a tool

If you have favorite macros you want to get at quickly, add them to a toolbar. To assign your macro to a tool on the toolbar:

1. Open the macro sheet containing the macro.

2. Display the toolbar to which you want to add your custom tool.

3. Choose the **O**ptions **T**oolbars command.

4. The Toolbars dialog is displayed. Choose the **C**ustomize button.

5. Select Custom from the **C**ategories list.

6. Drag one of the custom toolfaces onto a toolbar. When you drop the tool on a toolbar, the Assign To Tool dialog box appears.

7. Select the macro you want to run when this tool is clicked, then choose OK.

8. Choose Close.

The macro sheet containing the macros you have assigned to tools must be open for your custom tool to work. To ensure that the correct macro sheet is open when you run Excel, copy the macro sheet into the \EXCEL\XLSTART directory. This opens the macro sheet whenever you start Excel.

## Assign a different action to a built-in tool

Most tools in the Categories group of the Customize dialog box already have functions assigned to them. However, you can assign your own macro to any tool on any toolbar. Your macro will take precedence over the normal action for that tool.

To assign a macro to any tool:

1. Open the macro sheet or sheets that contain the macros you want to assign.

2. Display the Customize dialog box.

3. Click the tool you want to assign a macro to. Choose the Macro Assign to Tool command.

4. The Assign To Tool dialog box appears. Select the macro you want to run when this tool is clicked.

5. Choose OK.

6. Choose Close in the Customize dialog box if you do not need to assign additional tools.

## Set the default item in a dialog box

Most users want a dialog box to display so it is ready for them to enter their first selection. If the first data entry item is an edit box they want it selected so they can type. If it is a list, they want the list selected so they can immediately scroll through the list. To get this to work consistently, you need to know the following.

The first item you draw in the dialog editor that can be selected, such as an edit box or list, will be the default item when your custom dialog box is displayed. This first item will also be the first selectable item as you go down the rows in the dialog description table on the macro sheet.

For example, a text item may precede an edit box in the description table, but the edit box is the first selectable item.

What often throws off this simple rule is that the OK and Cancel buttons always attempt to be the default. When you add an OK or a Cancel button to a dialog box, make sure the Default check box in the Button dialog box is cleared. When you add the original OK and Cancel buttons to a box, the Default check box is selected. If you paste the default OK and Cancel buttons in the dialog box, they take precedence over the first selectable item in the dialog description table.

## Create moveable dialog boxes that include titles

Custom dialog boxes are friendlier and more informative if the user can drag them to another location on-screen and if they show a descriptive title. You can accomplish both tasks in the dialog editor. Double-click the background of the dialog box so the Dialog Info dialog box appears. In the Text box, type the title you want at the top of your dialog box. Dialog boxes that have a title will move.

If you have already created a dialog box and pasted it into a dialog description table on your macro sheet, you can still add a title and make it moveable. Enter your title in the text cell for the dialog box outline. The text cell for the dialog box is the sixth column of the first row. The first row describes the dialog box size. The sixth column contains text descriptions or displays.

## Move multiple items as a group when drawing in a dialog box

When you are drawing in the dialog editor, you may need to move a group of items together so they maintain their relative positions. You must do this, for example, when you resize the box or add items. To select multiple items and move them as a group, click the first item, then hold down the Shift key as you click additional items. Drag the group as a whole to its new location. Click the background of the dialog box to return to a single selection.

## Enter some functions as arrays to use them correctly

 Functions such as FILES, DIRECTORIES, DOCUMENTS, and WINDOWS are array functions. These functions return a horizontal array of results. Individual items in these arrays can be retrieved with an INDEX function. For example, INDEX(FILES,1,5) retrieves the name of the fifth file in the FILES array.

These arrays are not always straightforward. Sometimes, you must transpose a horizontal array into a vertical array. After the array is vertical, its contents can be used in a scrolling list of a custom dialog box.

Figure 12.1 shows a macro sheet in two windows. The macro sheet uses DOCUMENTS to read all the open documents so they can be displayed in a list in a custom dialog box. Choosing one of these document names from the list activates it. To transpose the horizontal array to a vertical array, you must use a trick.

A description of the code and dialog box is needed first. Beginning with the upper window, the dialog box is defined as Dlg.ShowFile in the range E2:K5. The K3 cell, named FileToActivate, contains the number of the item selected from the list. If the third item in the list is chosen, K3 and hence FileToActivate will be 3.

The lower window contains the macro that displays the dialog box described by the range Dlg.ShowFile. The

names in column A, Avail.Files and End, name the cells to
the right in column B. The formula in cell B10 sends the
macro to End if no document is open.

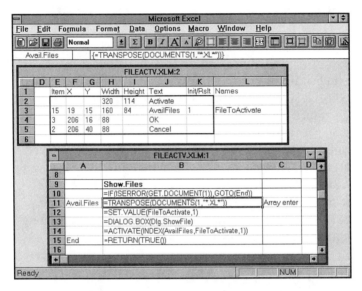

**Fig. 12.1** *Load arrays directly into scrolling list boxes.*

Here is the part that isn't in the manuals. The TRANSPOSE
function in cell B11 transposes the horizontal array returned by DOCUMENTS. But only the first document
named will be usable by the Avail.Files name unless you
enter the TRANSPOSE(DOCUMENTS()) formula as an
array. (Remember, when typing an array formula, you
press Ctrl+Shift+Enter to enter the braces, { and }. You
don't type the braces themselves.) This vertical list that
passes from the TRANSPOSE array into Avail.Files can
now be used in cell J3 as the contents for the scrolling
list box.

The SET.VALUE function sets the first choice in the list as
the default. The INDEX function selects the document

from the vertical Avail.Files list, and ACTIVATE activates the document.

## Use INDIRECT to work with calculated range names

Your macro will halt if you try to use text when Excel is expecting a reference. Figure 12.2 shows one way to handle this problem. In the example, a worksheet named NAMEDSHT.XLS contains columns named with the Formula Define Name command. The macro activates the worksheet, then starts at the top of the list of named ranges and selects in turn the columns named Col1, Col2, and Col3. This macro, or a variation, is useful for selecting a named set of ranges. After each range is selected, the macro pauses. Instead of pausing, the macro could be changed to define a print range and print or set up a data entry area (or perform any such repetitive action).

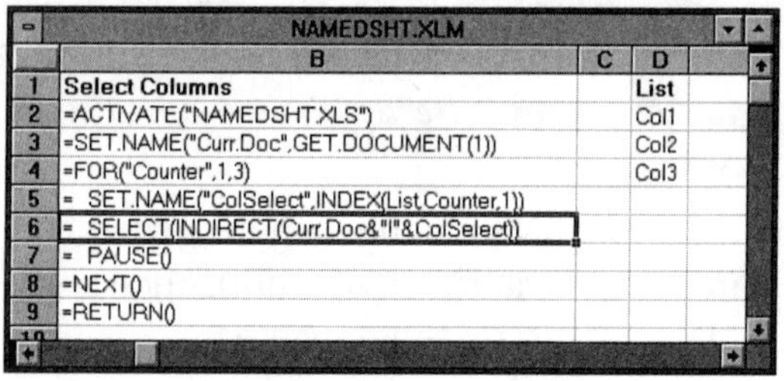
NAMEDSHT.XLM

| | B | C | D |
|---|---|---|---|
| 1 | Select Columns | | List |
| 2 | =ACTIVATE("NAMEDSHT.XLS") | | Col1 |
| 3 | =SET.NAME("Curr.Doc",GET.DOCUMENT(1)) | | Col2 |
| 4 | =FOR("Counter",1,3) | | Col3 |
| 5 | = SET.NAME("ColSelect",INDEX(List,Counter,1)) | | |
| 6 | = SELECT(INDIRECT(Curr.Doc&"!"&ColSelect)) | | |
| 7 | = PAUSE() | | |
| 8 | =NEXT() | | |
| 9 | =RETURN() | | |

**Fig. 12.2** *Use INDIRECT to convert text names and references to valid references.*

The macro begins by ensuring that the worksheet with the named columns is active. Cell B3 then stores the name of the active document in the name Curr.Doc. By using a variable name for the active document, you can use this macro with different active documents.

The FOR-NEXT loop in cells B4 and B8 loop through the list three times so that each column name will be used. SET.NAME stores the name for that pass through the loop, but the name is stored as text. This could cause a problem because the SELECT function in cell B6 expects to work on a reference, not text.

The INDIRECT function converts a full reference in text form to a valid reference. Because a full reference is needed, the document name, an exclamation mark, and the name of the column are concatenated. Each time through the loop, the column name is different, so a different column or columns are selected.

The PAUSE function pauses the macro after each time through the loop so you can see what was selected. Click the Resume tool to resume the macro when it is paused.

## Create scrolling lists that allow multiple selections

 Some types of scrolling lists beg the user to make multiple selections, such as multiple reports to print, multiple files to download from the mainframe, and multiple product names to enter in a table. But why keep displaying the dialog box over and over when you could make all the selections at one time?

The dialog box description table and macro in figure 12.3 show you how to enable multiple selections in a scrolling list, and how to handle the multiple selections the user makes. The dialog box description table is named Dlg.City and is in the range A3:G6. The list that is displayed in the dialog box is named List.Cities and is in the range F9:F18. The list of cities is loaded into the scrolling list by putting the name of the list in cell F4, the text column for the scrolling list.

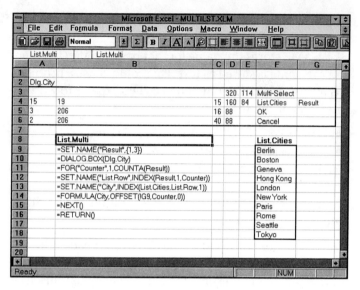

**Fig. 12.3** *Give your users the chance to make multiple selections.*

What tells the scrolling list to allow multiple selections is that cell G4, the Init/Result cell for the list, contains a name, Result. Normally the row number of the list item selected is put in the Init/Result cell for a scrolling list. But if a name is in this cell, Excel allows multiple selections with that name from the list. Excel stores in the name the row numbers of all items selected from the list. (You can use any valid name; it does not have to be Result.)

Cell B9 shows you how to set a default for the multiple selection list. Two numbers, 1 and 3, will be stored in the name Result. Because Result is in the Init/Result cell for the list, Excel selects the first and third items in the scrolling list when the dialog box first displays. Notice the braces typed around 1,3. This is one of the few times you can get by with typing braces. You do *not* have to enter this as an array by pressing Ctrl+Shift+Enter.

When the dialog box is displayed, you can hold down the Ctrl key and click multiple selections in the list. When you choose OK, the numbers of all the rows you selected are stored in Result. The FOR loop that starts in cell B11 counts how many numbers are in Result and loops that many times. Each time through the loop, the INDEX in B12 pulls out a row number from Result. Cell B13 then pulls the name of the city from that row number in List.Cities.

Finally, the FORMULA and OFFSET functions enter the city into a cell. The first entry is in a cell one down from cell G9 on the active worksheet or macro sheet. Each time through the loop, the COUNTER makes OFFSET put the city in the next row down.

## Use fancy titles in dialog boxes

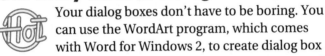 Your dialog boxes don't have to be boring. You can use the WordArt program, which comes with Word for Windows 2, to create dialog box titles. Figure 12.4 shows a dialog box using a title created in WordArt, the object that created the title, and the macro code that describes and displays the dialog box.

When you create your dialog box from the dialog editor, add a Picture icon as follows:

1. Choose the Item Icon command.

2. Select the Picture option and choose OK.

3. Stretch the picture icon that appears so it fits the dialog box as you want it. (A picture will not show in the picture icon.)

4. Complete the other elements of your dialog box.

5. Select and copy the dialog box, and paste the dialog description table on your macro sheet. Notice that

the picture icon appears as the word `Picture` in the text column of the dialog description table.

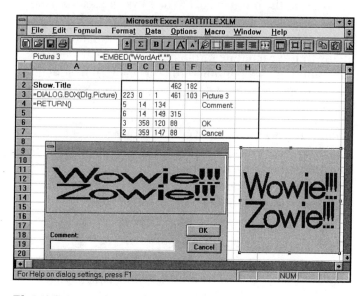

**Fig. 12.4** *Put any picture, chart, or drawing in your dialog box.*

Next, you need to create a drawing, picture, chart, or WordArt object to replace the picture icon in the dialog box. If you have Word for Windows 2, you can create a WordArt title.

To embed a WordArt object in your macro sheet:

1. Select a cell in your macro sheet.

2. Choose the Edit Insert **O**bject command.

3. From the **O**bject Type list, select MS WordArt. (If you want to draw a graphic, you can select Microsoft Drawing.)

4. Choose OK and the WordArt program appears.

5. Create a title in WordArt, then exit WordArt.

Your title appears on the macro sheet as a graphic object. While the object is selected, you can see its name in the Reference box at the top left of the screen. WordArt objects are Pictures, so you will see the word `Picture #`, where # is a number. Change the text in the dialog box description to match the object type and number. For example, cell G3 is Picture 3 because that is the name of the WordArt title in the lower right corner of the screen. Other graphic objects use other names, such as Chart 5.

# 13

## CHAPTER

# Customizing Excel

This chapter shows you tips for customizing the way Excel starts. One way is to learn a little about the EXCEL4.INI file, which is a text file you can edit with the Windows Notepad. Another way is to add icons in the Program Manager that start individual files in Excel.

### Use icons to start worksheets, macros, or charts

 In the Program Manager, you can assign your own icons that start Excel for a certain task and with a specific worksheet, macro sheet, or chart. Figure 13.1 shows a group window containing some Windows 3.1 and Excel 4 icons that you can use to start Excel worksheets, macros, or charts.

Before you assign specific Excel icons, you may want to create group windows in the Program Manager; each group window would contain icons related to a certain type of work. Follow these steps:

1. With the Program Manager active, choose the File New command.

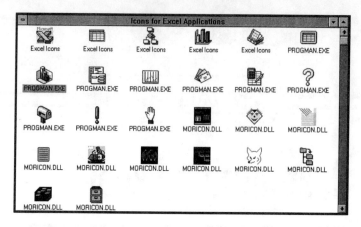

**Fig. 13.1** *Start Excel documents from icons.*

2. Select the Program **G**roup option.

3. Choose OK.

4. In the **D**escription edit box of the Program Group Properties dialog box, type the title you want to appear above your group window.

5. Choose OK.

To assign a specific worksheet or chart to an icon:

1. Activate the Program Manager, then activate the group window in which you want your icon.

2. Choose the **F**ile **N**ew command.

3. The New Program Object dialog box appears. Select the Program **I**tem option, then choose OK.

4. The Program Item Properties dialog box appears (see fig. 13.2). In the **D**escription text box, type the description you want to appear under the icon. Then choose the **B**rowse button.

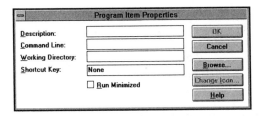

**Fig. 13.2** *Create your new icon and its description with this dialog box.*

5. The Browse dialog box appears. Find the EXCEL.EXE file (it's usually in the \EXCEL directory) and choose OK. This action enters in the Command Line the path and file used to start Excel.

6. If you want Excel to start with a worksheet, macro sheet, or chart, type a space at the end of the Command Line, followed by the path and file name of the worksheet, macro sheet, or chart you want to start.

7. If you want Excel to start in a specific directory (for example, the one containing the worksheet, macro sheet, or chart), type the path in the Working Directory edit box.

8. Choose the Change Icon button.

9. The Change Icon dialog box appears. This dialog box indicates the icons you can display in the Program Manager. (The icons shown in figure 13.3 are stored in the EXCEL.EXE file. Note that Windows 3.1 has other collections of icons.)

10. Select the icon you want from the Current Icon scrolling bar, then choose OK.

11. Choose OK to close the Program Item Properties dialog box.

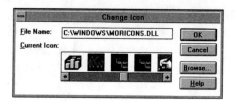

**Fig. 13.3** *Use this dialog box to select the icon you want to appear in the Program Manager.*

The icon you selected appears in the active group window. When you double-click the icon or select the icon and press Enter, Excel starts and the worksheet, chart, or macro you specified is loaded.

## Select from the Windows icon collections

Windows 3.1 has three collections of icons that are useful with Excel. When you are assigning an icon using the preceding tip, you can access the other icons available in Windows 3.1. Choose the Browse button from the Change Icon dialog box and select an EXE, DLL, or ICO file. The Windows 3.1 and Excel collections of icons are located in the following files:

`\EXCEL\EXCEL.EXE`

`\WINDOWS\PROGMAN.EXE`

`\WINDOWS\MORICONS.DLL`

Choose OK to enter the file name in the File Name edit box of the Change Icon dialog box shown in figure 13.3. Additional collections of icons can be purchased commercially, downloaded from many electronic bulletin boards, or drawn using icon drawing programs.

## Edit the EXCEL4.INI file to change Excel startup settings

When Excel starts, it reads the settings in the EXCEL4.INI file and uses them to set defaults and ancillary file locations. By changing this file, you can customize many of Excel's startup settings. (The Excel installation creates the EXCEL4.INI file in the same directory as the WIN.INI file, which is usually in the \WINDOWS directory.)

To change settings in the EXCEL4.INI file, start the Windows Notepad in the Accessories group. Use File Open to change to the \WINDOWS directory. Change the file pattern to *.INI and choose OK so you can see the INI files available. Open the EXCEL4.INI file. Immediately save this file with the name EXCEL4.BAK. In this way, if you enter something incorrectly in EXCEL4.INI, you can return Excel to its original condition by exiting Windows and from the DOS prompt typing a command such as

```
COPY C:\WINDOWS\EXCEL4.BAK C:\WINDOWS\EXCEL4.INI
```

This action replaces the INI file with a copy of the original.

Use the editing features of the Notepad to change the settings in EXCEL4.INI. When you are finished making changes, save the file to its original directory with the name EXCEL4.INI. If you are using a word processor, this file must be saved as a text file. Notepad automatically saves files in the text format.

## Indicate files you want opened on startup

Use the EXCEL4.INI file to designate files you want opened on startup. This enables you to start files without placing them in the XLSTART directory. You can also use startup switches on these files.

To indicate a file to open on startup, you can add lines such as the following:

```
OPEN1= C:\EXPENSES\PERSONAL.XLS

OPEN2= /r C:\EXPENSES\FORM.XLS

OPEN3= /f C:\EXPENSES\EXPFNCTN.XLM
```

If you have a single OPEN statement, use the word OPEN.
If you have multiple files to OPEN, number each one as
shown here.

When you use the /r switch, the file opens as read only.
When you use the /f switch, the function macros on the
specified macro sheet are added to the User Defined category of the Paste Functions dialog box. This makes the
function macros available to the user when Excel starts,
just as though the functions were a built-in part of Excel.

## Set the default font

Use the FONT command to specify the default font for
new worksheets, row and column headings, and information in the Info window. Enter the FONT command in the
EXCEL4.INI file as described in previous tips. If you want
to change many startup settings in the startup worksheet,
use a startup worksheet in the XLSTART directory as described in Chapter 1.

Make sure that you spell the font exactly as it appears
in the font dialog box. Use an available font size. For
example, to start Excel with the a 9-point Arial font, use

```
FONT=Arial,9
```

## Control Excel's startup window size

If you want Excel to start in a maximized window, add the
following line in the EXCEL4.INI file:

```
Maximized=1
```

To start Excel in a floating window, use

```
Maximized=0
```

# 14

# Finding Other Sources of Help

There are many avenues of support for Microsoft Excel in addition to using Excel's help feature. People and resources are available to train you, to answer your questions by phone or FAX, to help you learn more on your own, and even to develop applications using Excel worksheets and its extensive macro programming language.

## Use Microsoft's telephone support

Microsoft maintains telephone support for its products from 6 A.M. to 6 P.M., Pacific Daylight Time. If you call any of the phone numbers listed here, you usually will be asked whether you want to hear recorded tips for the most frequently asked questions or whether you want to speak directly to a support person. Microsoft has more than 1,200 support people.

Some technical support numbers you may find useful follow:

Directory of Product Support Numbers: 206-454-2030

Sales and Services (upgrades and interim releases): 800-426-9400

Windows 3.1: 206-637-7098

Excel for Windows: 206-635-7070

Word for Windows: 206-462-9673

TDD/TT (Telecommunications Device for the Deaf/Teletype): 206-635-4948

## Use Microsoft's automated voice and FAX support

Answers to many of the most frequently asked questions about Excel 3 and 4 are available 24 hours a day through Microsoft's automated support system. You can listen to a voice description of questions and answers. At the end of each sequence, you can request a FAX containing the full response. The FAX usually is sent within a few hours. Contact the automated support services at the following numbers:

Excel for Windows: 206-635-7071

Windows: 206-635-7245

## Use Microsoft OnLine for drivers and files

If you need application notes or software drivers other than those on the original installation disks, you can download them through the Microsoft OnLine service. The service also lists telephone support numbers for all Microsoft products.

To access the OnLine service, you need a modem and communications software. The OnLine telephone number is 206-936-6735. Communications settings for OnLine are

| | |
|---|---|
| Baud rate | 1200, 2400, or 9600 |
| Data bits | 8 |
| Stop bit | 1 |
| Parity | None |

The data bits, stop bit, and parity are the default settings for Windows Terminal, the communications package provided with Windows 3.1. Use the baud rate recommended for your modem.

## Access CompuServe forums

CompuServe is a public database and bulletin board service that stores business, medical, scientific, and personal information on many topics. If you are a CompuServe member, you can gain access to Microsoft databases, forums (bulletin boards), and libraries relating to Excel and other Microsoft products. Type one of the following CompuServe commands after the CompuServe ! prompt.

| | |
|---|---|
| GO MSOFT | The main menu to all Microsoft services on CompuServe |
| GO MSEXCEL | The menu for all forums and libraries related to Excel |
| GO MSKB | The menu to the Microsoft Knowledge Base, which contains answers to many of the problems that Microsoft's telephone support people encounter |
| GO MSL | The main menu for the Software Library |

To connect your computer to CompuServe, you need a CompuServe account, a modem, and communications software. For communications software, you can use the Terminal program provided with Windows. CompuServe has an inexpensive Windows program, WinCIM, that makes searching and downloading information much easier. To get an introductory membership to CompuServe or for information on WinCIM, call 800-848-8199.

## Get user training

Microsoft certifies training centers for introductory and intermediate level training on Windows and Excel. For information about your nearest authorized training center, call Microsoft sales and services at 800-426-9400. Skip the numeric phone tree by pressing 0 and asking the operator for Authorized Training Centers.

## Get advanced training or corporate consulting and application development

Microsoft maintains a Consultant Relations Program for consultants who develop applications with specific Microsoft products. Consultants must take certification exams, submit applications for code review, and submit a list of clients. The highest level of consultant is the Microsoft Consulting Partner.

Ron Person, the author of this book, is one of the original Microsoft Excel and Word for Windows Consulting Partners, and is the best-selling author of the following Que titles: *Using Excel 4 for Windows*, Special Edition, *Using Windows 3.1*, Special Edition, and *Using Word for Windows*, Special Edition.

Ron Person & Co. develops applications and trains support personnel and programmers for corporations nationwide. He trains developers in the use of Excel's macro language and the Microsoft Open EIS Pak. The firm has developed applications for Fortune 1000 corporations in the areas of marketing, finance, and human resources. For more information, write to the following address:

Ron Person
Ron Person & Co.
3 Quixote Ct.
Santa Rosa, CA 95409

707-539-1525   Voice
415-989-7508   Voice
707-538-1485   Fax

## Purchase other books

A book is one of the easiest and least expensive ways to learn more about Excel. Another helpful book on Excel by Ron Person (in addition to the one you're reading now) is *Using Excel 4 for Windows,* Special Edition (by Que Corporation). This 1141-page book, an international best-seller, is a comprehensive book on Excel, beginning with the basics and continuing through creating custom dialog boxes with macros. It includes all Excel features and add-ins, hundreds of tips, and many real-world examples.

*Excel Trade Secrets for Windows* by Reed Jacobson reveals many of the tips and tricks Reed has learned in his years as a Microsoft Consulting Partner in Excel. This 728-page book and its accompanying disk show how to combine features in Excel to create more power. The book includes complete coverage of creating reports, working with mainframe text files, and converting Lotus 1-2-3 files. Developers will appreciate some of the added capabilities and tools Reed has developed with macros.

# Index

## H

headers, 133-135
height, rows, 128
help files, 180-181
Help tool, 38
hiding columns/rows,
 123-125
holidays, 72-74
horizontal
 arrays, 186
 titles, 135-136

## I-K

icons
 accessing, 198
 defining, 195-198
IF formula, 127, 128
IF function, 71-72
increasing
 line spacing, 128, 129
 row height, 128
INDEX function, 74-75
INDIRECT function, 189
inserting
 cells, 27-29
 columns, 27-29
 rows, 27-29

keypad, 75
keys, *see* shortcut keys

## L

labels, 127-128
legends, 158-159, 168-169
limiting crosstab reports, 118
limiting data analysis, 117-118
lines
 charts, symbols, 156-157
 spacing, 128-129

linking
 floating text blocks,
  159-160
 formulas with worksheets,
  106
 worksheet numbers,
  159-160
locating cells, 146-147
Lotus 1-2-3 files
 converting, 205
 format, 53

## M

macro sheets, 5-6
macros
 assigning
  to tools, 183-184
  to graphics, 181-182
 codes, reading, 179-180
 data entry, 175-178
 debugging, 174
 displaying, 171-172
 sections, deactivating, 174
 starting, 195-198
 STRUCTM.XLT, 179-180
 tools, 42
 troubleshooting, 178
 uppercase, 172
margins, 137-138
markers, selecting, 156
MATCH function, 74-75
maximized windows, 200
menus, shortcut, 15-17
Microsoft Excel telephone
 support, 201-202
Microsoft OnLine service,
 202-203
Microsoft Open EIS Pak, 180,
 205

printing
  enlarging, 138
  formulas, 103-104
  margins, editing, 137-138
  outlines, data, 131-132
  pages, sizing, 138
  reducing, 138
  restricted outlines, 115-116
  selected data, 131-132
  setting, 132-133
  titles, 136
  tools, 40
Program Manager, 62
protecting
  formulas, 75-76
  ranges, 29-30
  worksheets, 76-77

## Q-R

queries, calculating, 144-146

range names
  calculated, 188-189
  lowercase, 172-173
ranges
  data
    calculating, 108-110
    naming, 160-165
  filling with formulas or
    data, 17-20
  formats, 69-70
  naming, 33-34
  protecting, 29-30
  saving, 132-133
  selecting
    View Manager, 34-36
    with Goto dialog box,
      22-23

reading codes, macros,
  179-180
recalculating
  crosstab reports, 119
  formulas, 99-100
redefining databases, 141
reducing
  print size, 138
  size of worksheets, 23
references
  calculating, 142
  cell, 95, 144
  circular, 104-106
relative cell references, 95
removing documents from
  workbooks, 8, 10
repeating titles, multiple
  pages, 135-136
reports
  breaks, 126-127
  creating, 123, 147-150
  extracting data, 147-150
  subtotals, 125-129
  writing, 123-129
resetting toolbars, 45-46
restricted outlines, printing,
  115-116
retitling legends, 168-169
retrieving crosstab report
  data, 119-120
rotating charts, 153-154
rows
  deleting, 28-29
  displaying, 87, 123-125
  height, 128
  hiding, 87, 123-125
  inserting, 27-29
  totaling, 107

## S

saving
  files, 7-8
  ranges, 132-133
  toolbars, 48-49
scaling charts, 170
Scenario Manager, 113-115
scrolling lists, multiple
  selections, 189-191
sections, macros,
  deactivating, 174
seed date, 57
Select as Displayed tool,
  115-116
selecting
  areas, 23
  arguments, 98-99
  buttons, 182
  cells, 25-36
  chart data, 156
  data to print, 131-132
  databases, 141
  formulas, 98-99
  ranges, 22-23
  single markers, 156
sending files as single
  documents, 8
settings
  print, 132-133
  startup, 199
SHEET.XLT template, 4
shortcut keys
  built-in, 172
  Current date (Ctrl+;
    (semicolon)), 51-52
  entering current date and
    time, 51-52
  entering data in multiple
    cells (Ctrl+Enter), 52

filling cells (Ctrl+Enter),
  17-18
Goto (F5), 21-22
numeric format, 89
shortcut menus
  accessing, 15-17
  Toolbar, 37
single array formulas, 108-110
single markers, selecting, 156
sizing
  pages, 138
  worksheets, 23
software, communication,
  203
Solitaire, 49-50
Sort name, 143
sort ranges, 142-144
sorting databases, 139-140
special characters, 61-64
spell check, 65-68, 150-151
splitting windows, 182-183
Standard toolbars, 44
starting
  charts, 195-198
  macros, 195-198
  worksheets, 195-198
startup
  files, opening, 199-200
  opening documents
    automatically, 3
  settings, 199
  worksheets, 4-5
STEP function, 173-174
STRUCTM.XLT macro,
  179-180
styles, 85-86
  cells, 84-85
  Normal, 88
  worksheets, 86

## U–V

uppercase macros, 172
user support, 201-202

value axis, 157-170
values
    cells, copying, 52
    formulas, 68
vertical
    arrays, 186
    axis, 157
    titles, 135-136
View Manager, 34-36, 132-133
viewing buttons, 182-183

## W

wedges, pie chart, 156
white space, 129
width
    cells, 107-111
    columns, 137-138
Windows Paintbrush, 47-48
windows
    floating, 200
    maximized, 200
    splitting, 182-183
Word for Windows Equation Editor, 64-65
WordArt program, 191-193
work days, checking, 72-74
workbooks, 8-10

worksheets
    cells, naming, 114-115
    checking spelling, 65
    data, transferring, 178
    embedding equations, 64-65
    entries, 53
    formatting, 82-83
    formulas
        linking, 106
        multiple, 99
        pasting, 100-101
        printing, 103-104
        recalculating, 99-100
    group edit, 28-29, 53
    navigatiing, 32
    numbers, 159-160
    protecting, 76-77
    reducing size, 23
    results, 171
    starting, 195-198
    startup, 4-5
    styles, 86
    summary information, 11-12
    templates, 5-6
writing reports, 123-129

## X-Z

Y-axis, 157

Zoom feature, 23